DUBLIN

Contents

Written by Teresa Fisher

Updated by Anto Howard

American editor Tracy Larson

Edited, designed and produced by AA Publishing
© Automobile Association Developments Limited 2005, 2007
Maps © Automobile Association Developments Limited 2005, 2007
This edition first published in the United States 2006

Maps based on Ordnance Survey Ireland Permit No. 7954
© Ordnance Survey Ireland and Government of Ireland

Published in the United States by AAA Publishing,
1000 AAA Drive, Heathrow, Florida 32746-5063
Published in the United Kingdom by AA Publishing

ISBN 978-1-59508-236-7

Cover design and binding style by permission of AA Publishing
Color separation by Keenes, Andover
Printed and bound in China by Leo Paper Products

10 9 8 7 6 5 4 3 2 1

A03183
Maps based on Ordnance Survey Ireland Permit No. 8136
© Ordnance Survey Ireland and Government of Ireland

the magazine

There's no denying – Dublin has come of age. Local writer Brendan Behan once described the city as "th largest village in Europe", while for James Joyce, "dear dirty Dublin" was the key to understanding all the other cities of the world. In many ways both were right. Dublin is both parochial and cosmopolitan; intimate yet global in outlook; traditional ye full of contemporary flair; a village c a million-plus inhabitants and a bustling metropolis.

Previous page and above: St Patrick's Day Parade

Dublin

Today's "fair city" oozes confidence as the increasingly fashionable capital of a young, independent, democratic Republic, no longer living on its Georgian past and dominated by the puritanical spirit of Irish Catholicism. Over the years it has been reinvented by U2, Colin Farrell, Roddy Doyle and Riverdance to become a vibrant and fun-loving boomtown, consciously European in outlook, abuzz with sophisticated bars, restaurants, clubs and shops, and basking in the prestige and revenue of its world-class museums and galleries. "City of a thousand pubs and a thousand bands", "capital of Euro-cool", "The Literary Giant", "party capital of Europe" – the list of epithets goes on…No wonder Dublin

Right: Laid back in Temple Bar

Below: 21st-century city

ranks among Europe's favourite holiday destinations. The capital's profound trans-

formation is mainly due to its major economic development. Since 1994 the Irish economy has sustained a staggering average annual growth of more than 7 per cent – the highest in the European Union – prompting the British journal *The Economist* to coin the term "Celtic Tiger". Dublin is now a world-class banking centre, the London–Dublin air route is the fourth busiest in the world and, with Ireland as the world's second largest exporter of software, the government is striving to establish the capital as the "e-commerce" hub of Europe.

walk the streets to see the cranes on the horizon, the modern architecture and the extraordinary number of new hotels, pubs and restaurants as the city powers ahead with new buildings and restoration projects.

But Dublin's economic miracle also has negative ramifications. Prices have increased dramatically – most noticeably in the housing market – and traffic congestion is a growing problem. Ironically for a nation with a tradition of emigration, the capital is only slowly getting to grips with its own nascent

Today

The success of the Celtic Tiger, combined with the youngest population in Europe (40 per cent under 25 years of age) and the huge growth in the number of immigrants and visitors, has led to increased prosperity and transformed Dublin into a truly international city.
You only have to

multi-culturalism, following the dramatic influx of immigrants, who have brought with them vibrant cultures often at odds with Dublin's own.

Despite the changes, the new Dublin has been careful not to replace the old Dublin. The city has reinvented itself but, at the same time, it has retained its inimitable character, carefully preserving everything that makes it unique. With its clever blend of urban dynamism and rural charm, there is still nowhere quite like it.

The essence of the Irish capital and its people hasn't really changed: the Dubliners' well-deserved reputation for friendliness, wit and irrepressible sense of fun remains. You can

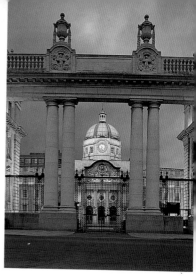

and *Guinness* is still good for you!

Perhaps the most subtle

"CITY OF A THOUSAND PUBS AND A THOUSAND BANDS"

still find a quiet pub to while away a few hours where, if you are lucky, traditional musicians

may be playing for free; take pleasure in the classical symmetry of an elegant Georgian square, or admire the views along the Liffey quays;

change is the emergence of a new breed of Dubliners – typically young, confident and educated – who have realised their worth on the world market. Their powerful pride of place is almost tangible; their love of their city remains constant no matter how much it changes.

There has never been a more exciting time to visit Dublin. As the city continues to develop, it still retains that essential and unique Dublin feel, blending tradition with the ever-changing pace of contemporary life in Ireland today. The feel-good factor in the capital is high, and the "tiger" continues to roar…

Above: The Dail – seat of the Irish Parliament

The Craic

People come to Dublin in search of it, and everywhere you go you'll hear people talking about it – *craic* (pronounced "crack"). Hard to define, in essence it means "a good time". It can happen anywhere or anytime. It's a mood, something in the air… people, places and events can all be "great *craic*".

Craic usually contains one or more of the following: music, friends old or new, lively chat, dancing, food, drink, plenty of laughter and an unmistakably Irish atmosphere. The best place to experience the *craic* is the Irish pub. With more than 800 pubs listed in the phone book, Dublin boasts the greatest concentration of real, old-fashioned pubs anywhere in the world, so you're sure to find some "mighty good *craic*". Even though the city is developing fast, the pub remains the heart of its social life, where locals spend hours swapping stories and gossip, enjoying a *Guinness* and perhaps an impromptu music session. But the *craic* doesn't have to be restricted to a pub. It can be anywhere if the ingredients are right…

THE CRAIC

" …So then the door flies open and in comes a man fit for dancing and he gets up on the floor there and starts into the jig. By this time there's a fiddle going and the whole room dancing… Fierce nice! Ah, the craic was mighty, all right…"
(A musician in conversation)

Poets & Storytellers

Scene from Jonathan Swift's celebrated novel *Gulliver's Travels*

Considering its small size, Dublin has produced more than its fair share of celebrated writers. Four Nobel Prizes for literature have been awarded to its progeny – George Bernard Shaw, William Butler Yeats, Samuel Beckett and Seamus Heaney – and there have been numerous other luminaries. Dublin's great writing tradition, nurtured for centuries in the nicotine-stained bars, seems to infiltrate every corner of the city. As soon as you arrive, the ghosts of James Joyce, Brendan Behan and Oscar Wilde sweep you along on a tide of literary consciousness – with Dublin's overcrowded bars, colloquial conversations, decaying tenements and Georgian façades as stage sets for the city's larger-than-life drama.

DUBLIN AND EAST TOURISM

BRAM STOKER
1847 – 1912
THEATRE MANAGER
AUTHOR OF DRACULA
LIVED HERE

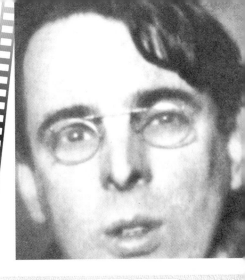

The Irish literary tradition dates back to early Gaelic civilisations, through troubadour songs and manuscripts preserved by monks and poets. The *Book of Kells*, (► 91–92), with its elaborate illuminations, is an exceptional example of Ireland's early reverence for words.

The first great Irish writer in English was the satirist

Above: William Butler Yeats, a leader of the Irish Renaissance

Jonathan Swift (► 23), a graduate of Trinity College and author of the allegorical *Gulliver's Travels* (1726), which has become a children's classic. **George Farquhar** (*c*1677–1707), a contemporary of Swift, sacrificed acting to become a playwright after accidentally wounding a fellow actor with a sword. His most successful restoration comedies, *The Beaux Stratagem* and *The Recruiting Officer*, are still popular today. In the mid-19th century, novelists **Joseph Sheridan Le Fanu** (1814–73) and **Bram Stoker** (1847–1912), both Dublin-born, came to the fore with their new genre of horror. After his wife died in 1858, Le Fanu became a recluse, known to his friends as "the Invisible Prince". He wrote his most famous works, *Uncle Silas* and *The House by the Churchyard,* in bed between the hours of midnight and dawn in an attempt to exorcise his increasing obsession with death and the supernatural. Inspired by Le Fanu, Stoker began his literary career as an unpaid drama critic on the *Dublin Evening Mail*. His masterwork, *Dracula*, was moderately well received but following its posthumous dramatisation in 1924 it became a resounding success.

Nineteenth-century refinement could be observed in the sophisticated social plays of **George Bernard Shaw** (► 75 and 95), including *Pygmalion, Saint Joan* and *Arms and the*

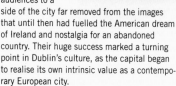

RODDY DOYLE

Roddy Doyle's trilogy – *The Commitments, The Snapper* and *The Van* – about working-class life in Dublin, introduced international audiences to a side of the city far removed from the images that until then had fuelled the American dream of Ireland and nostalgia for an abandoned country. Their huge success marked a turning point in Dublin's culture, as the capital began to realise its own intrinsic value as a contemporary European city.

Man; and in those of Irish wit, poet and dramatist **Oscar Wilde** (► 107), whose worldwide fame rests on such comic masterpieces as *Lady Windermere's Fan, An Ideal Husband* and *The Importance of Being Earnest*. Both Dublin-born, their plays dominated the theatre on both sides of the Irish Sea from the 1880s until World War II. This period marked the Golden Age of Dublin literature, and Shaw was awarded the Nobel

LITERARY PUBS

Brendan Behan and Patrick Kavanagh used to frequent the **Duke** (► 87).
• **McDaid's** (► 116) was popular with Behan, Kavanagh and Flann O'Brien. It was also a setting for James Joyce's story *Grace*.
• Flann O'Brien was also a patron of **Neary's** (► 160).
• The **Stag's Head** (► 159–160) was a regular haunt of Joyce.
• **Toner's** (► 113 and 161) was the only pub William Butler Yeats ever entered.
• **Davy Byrne's** (► 112 and 160) was where Joyce's hero Bloom had a gorgonzola cheese sandwich and a glass of burgundy for lunch in *Ulysses*.

Prize for literature in 1925. But it was **W B Yeats** (1865–1939), a member of the Irish Free State Senate and the Irish Republican Brotherhood (a forerunner of the IRA) who best captured the restless, yearning spirit of Irish nationalism in such plays as *Cathleen ni Houlihan* and the poem *Easter 1916*, with its immortal line "All changed, changed utterly: A terrible beauty is born." His reputation rests more on his poetry, for which he received the Nobel Prize for literature in 1923.

Yeats hailed **Sean O'Casey** (1880–1964) as one of Ireland's great literary geniuses. His first plays – *The Shadow of a Gunman, Juno and the Paycock* and *The Plough and the Stars* – illustrating how the real victims of the civil war had been the civilians, proved too close to the truth for comfort, causing audiences to riot at their premières. As a consequence, O'Casey chose voluntary exile in England.

James Joyce (1882–1941) celebrated the character of Dublin more than any other Irish author, in works such as *The Dubliners* (a collection of short stories), *A Portrait of the Artist as a Young Man* and, his finest achievement, the epic *Ulysses* (► 31), which has linked his name forever with that of his home town. Joyce himself said of *Ulysses*: "I want to give a picture of Dublin so complete that if the city one day suddenly disappeared from the earth it could be reconstructed out of my book."

Other protégés of post-war Dublin include the Nobel Prize-winning dramatist, novelist and friend of Joyce **Samuel Beckett** (► 92); poet **Patrick Kavanagh**; and **Brendan Behan** – author, anti-English rebel and alcoholic from the age of eight. Popular novelists include **C S Lewis**, **Edna O'Brien**, **Flann O'Brien**, **J P Donleavy**, **Maeve Binchy** and Booker Prize-winners **Roddy Doyle** and **John Banville**, all of whom have immortalised aspects of Ireland in their best-selling books.

Left: Bronze of James Joyce

...a true Dubliner is said to be someone who is born between the two canals – the Royal on the Northside and the Grand on the Southside.

...Dublin owes its name to water – the original Viking name *Dubh Linn* meant "Black Pool" (▶ 65) and the city's Irish name, *Baile Átha Cliath*, means "Town of the Hurdle Ford" after the primitive system of stones and logs once erected there to prevent flooding.

...St Patrick (▶ 23), the patron saint of Ireland, isn't Irish! He was sent over from Britain as a Christian missionary to convert the island's Celtic pagans.

BET YOU DIDN'

...in 1800 the Irish Parliament in Dublin became the only parliament in history to vote itself out of existence (▶ 104).

...each year the Guinness Brewery receives more than 2,000 enquiries from people hoping to open a pub, and on average one Irish-themed pub opens every day somewhere in the world.

...a recipe for "roast child" was published in Dublin in 1729 as part of Jonathan Swift's *Modest Proposal*, an ironic attack against economics.

...the boisterous Dublin intellectual, novelist, dramatist and ballad singer Brendan Behan (left) claimed to have been thrown out of every pub in town!

Right: Brass plaques mark the city's James Joyce walk

14 *the magazine*

...the Liffey is a tidal river and its depth varies enormously with the movement of the tides. In summer months, when the tide is low, locals call it the "sniffey" or "whiffey" Liffey. In winter it can freeze over, and has been known to do so twice – in 1338 and in 1739.

patients "feel better, eat better, and think cheerfully".

...it takes time – no less than 119.5 seconds – for a pint of *Guinness* to settle properly, and to rush the process is to do this celebrated drink an injustice.

...a female cook was boiled alive on St Stephen's Green in 1773 for poisoning several people.

...Dublin's first aerial passenger – a cat – took off by balloon for the Isle

NOW THAT...

...James Joyce made up countless names for Dublin in his classic novel *Finnegans Wake*, including Dubbyling, Dublovnik, Tumblin on the Leafy, The Heart of MidLeinster, Londub, Babbalong, Eblana Magna, Old Brawn, Hurdlebury Finn and Dungbin.

...Dublin doctors used to prescribe *Guinness*, believing it made

of Man in 1784, followed months later by a human, Richard Crosbie, who made it only to Clontarf.

...a spark from a horseshoe ignited a pile of gunpowder by the Liffey docks in 1596, blowing up 120 people.

...in 1197 Dublin was excommunicated by the Pope following a quarrel with King John.

...like the rest of the nation, Dubliners love their potatoes. They eat 44 million tonnes per year.

Oysters &

GUINNESS.

I t's an exciting time in the development of Ireland's cuisine. The past decade in Dublin has seen the emergence of a vibrant and cosmopolitan food culture, with dozens of fashionable, new restaurants serving global cuisine – a trend that mirrors the extraordinary energy and innovation currently pulsing through the capital. Amid this culinary revolution, the simple dishes and straightforward flavours of Ireland's traditional country cooking remain constant but, now it has come of age gastronomically, it has the self-confidence to be proud of its culinary heritage. As a consequence, Irish cuisine is becoming more creative and is currently experiencing a renaissance.

Traditional Irish Cuisine

The appeal of traditional Irish cuisine is its hearty, unadulterated wholesomeness, the cooking of a primarily agricultural society, its main purpose to nourish and sustain. In this island nation, fish is the mainstay of the Irish table, together with meat and dairy produce, a wide range of breads, cakes and puddings, and a well-stocked basket

of fruit and vegetables. Typical dishes you are likely to find in the capital include the quintessential Irish dish – **rish stew** (a casserole made with mutton or lamb, onions and potatoes); **Dublin coddle** (boiled sausages, bacon, onions and potatoes in a thickened sauce); **boxties** (Irish potato pancakes with various savoury fillings); plenty of **lamb**,

fish and **seafood** dishes (fresh and smoked salmon, Dublin Bay prawns, oysters – often consumed with *Guinness*); **baked ham** roasted with cloves and brown sugar and commonly served with boiled cabbage; beef and stout casseroles; with mountains of **fresh vegetables** (leeks, carrots, potatoes of every shape, texture and size) and a huge variety of

Top chef Patrick Guilbaud

Irish cheeses (► 115). Irish breads and cakes are also especially tasty: try the **soda bread**, **scones** and **barm brack** (a doughy, fruity tea bread), the **apple tarts** and **porter cake** (a dark fruit cake famous for the inclusion of stout, usually *Guinness*). **Irish coffee** (coffee, cream and whiskey), of course, makes perfect end to any meal.

New Irish Cuisine

The best cooks in the city have moved away from the heaviness of traditional Irish cooking, favouring a lighter, more creative style. The resulting "New Irish Cuisine" – modern, experimental dishes **infusing flavours colours and culinary styles**, but based on the finest of Irish produce and still reflecting traditional themes – has taken the Dublin restaurant scene by storm. Now c menus, you can find such typical Dublin staples as coddle, traditionally a hotpot c sausage and bacon, reborn as a shellfish coddle; black pudding may be accompanied by a blue cheese and cider sorbet;

Traditional Irish Cuisine
~
Dublin Coddle
~

(Serves 4)
- 4 bacon rashers, cut in strips
- 2 large onions, coarsely sliced
- 2 crushed garlic cloves
- 8 large pork sausages
- 4 large potatoes, thinly sliced
- ¼ teaspoon dried sage
- 300ml chicken stock

Fry the bacon then add the onions and garlic and cook until golden. Fry the pork sausages for 5–6 minutes, until golden brown. Arrange the potatoes in a buttered ovenproof dish and place the other ingredients on top. Sprinkle with sage and add the stock. Cover and cook in the oven for 1 hour at Gas Mark 4, or 180°C/350°F.

TIME FOR A TIPPL

I
t is hardly surprising that the Irish a
reputedly fond of a tipple if you con
sider the fine quality of their native
drinks. During your stay, try the followin
- A good **stout**, such as *Guinness*, Murphy's or Darcy's.
- **Whiskey**, a traditional chaser to a dr of the "black stuff", is stored in oak v for at least three years, and often con siderably longer, to give it its smooth and distinctive flavour.
- **Baileys**, among the most popular liqueurs in the world, made from two Ireland's finest products – whiskey a cream. One variation is a "baby-*Guinness*" – a shot of kahlua with a creamy head of Baileys.

BEST NEW IRISH CUISINE

...uinness may find itself used as a ...bayon, coating a tender steak as ...pposed to the usual hearty beef ...d stout stew; and oysters may be ...rved with rice wine!

Leading exponents of new ...ish cuisine include Kevin ...hornton, Patrick Guilbaud and ...erry Clark. Together with con-...rns such as *Bord Bia* (the Irish ...od Board) – organisers of *Feile* ...a, a week-long festival of Irish ...od held each June – they are ...tively encouraging up-and-com-...g Irish chefs to pay homage to ...adition in their contemporary ...isine, and to bring real Irish ...avour into Dublin's restaurants. ...s they say in Irish, *Blas agus ...samh go bhfaighe tu air* (May ...ou find it both tasty and ...tisfying)!

New Irish Cuisine
Apple and Whiskey Tart

(Makes 4 individual tarts)

250g (8oz) shortcrust pastry
50g (2oz) ground almonds
4 large cooking apples,
    peeled and diced
2 tablespoons sugar
250ml (8fl oz) cream
3 egg yolks
50g (2oz) caster sugar
dash of whiskey

Line four tart tins with the pastry then sprinkle the almonds on to the base and add the apple. Heat the cream, beat the egg yolks and sugar together, then stir in the cream and a dash of whiskey.

Spoon a little of the cream mixture into each tart and bake for 20–25 minutes (Gas Mark 6, or 200°C/400°F). Pour the remaining cream mixture into a bowl, place in a bain marie, and stir constantly until the custard thickens. Serve with the tarts.

*F*ew people associate Dublin with parks and gardens, yet there are a surprising number of green spaces for recreation and ornamentation within the city centre catering for the needs of Dubliners who now, more than ever, seek respite from the increasing pace of urban life and a natural antidote to its noise, stress and congestion.

Most people relax in **Phoenix Park** (➤ 122–124), one of the world's largest urban parks, with its lush parkland, ancient oak trees, wild deer, memorials and zoo. Others snatch a ten-minute stroll or spend their lunch hour in **Archbishop Ryan Park**, the elegant gardens of **Merrion Square** (➤ 106–107), with its dazzling floral displays and unusual collection of old Dublin city lampposts; or in **St Stephen's Green** (➤ 100–103), a surprisingly serene park in the centre of town, with duck ponds, fountains and formal flowerbeds.

But those in the know head to quiet, understated **Iveagh Gardens**, one of the city's finest parks yet surprisingly one of the least well known, situated just a stone's throw from St Stephen's Green (the main entrance is in Clonmel Street). It was originally the private walled grounds of nearby Clonmel House, owned by the Guinness family until 1940. With its maze, grotto, fountains, rose gardens and woodlands, this wild,

unkempt park makes you feel you've escaped Dublin altogether.

Secret Gardens

For a quick dose of greenery in the city centre, make for the statue-filled little park attached to St Patrick's Cathedral, or **St Audoen's Park**, a small, leafy park adjoining St Audoen's Protestant church near Christ

& Quiet

…hurch Cathedral, bounded …the medieval city wall and …tes. On the Northside, just …minutes' from O'Connell …reet, the former city reser-…ir of **Blessington Street …sin**, commonly described …Dublin's "secret garden", is …w a quiet haven for both …sitors and local wildlife, and …akes a pleasant venue for a …fy stroll.

In the northern suburbs, magnificent **St Anne's Park and Rose Gardens** was once part of the home of the Guinness family of brewing fame. It is now a public park, with extensive woodlands, hidden walled gardens, tree-lined walks, an ornamental lake area and glorious rose gardens – best viewed between June and September.

St Stephen's Green – a veritable oasis of peace

Just beyond, **North Bull Island** in Dublin Bay is a nature reserve and bird sanctuary of international importance, with up to 25,000 wading birds resident here in winter, and great beach walks all year round.

Above: St Anne's Park and Rose Gardens

Remembrance Gardens
The **War Memorial Gardens**, on the southern banks of the Liffey facing Phoenix Park, are dedicated to the memory of the 49,000 Irish soldiers who died in World War I. Designed by English architect Sir Edwin Lutyens, they are a must-see for visitors interested in both gardens and architecture.

The **Garden of Remembrance** at the northern end of Parnell Square was opened in 1966 on the 50th anniversary of the Easter Rising (▶ 54), and is dedicated to all those who died for the cause of Irish independence. Ironically, the Easter Rising was plotted in a house nearby and the captured rebels were held prisoner in this square overnight. The garden is laid out around a sunken, cross-shaped pool, and is intended as a place of quiet contemplation and reflection. The large bronze *Children of Lír* sculpture by Oisín Kelly at the far end of the park alludes to ancient Irish myth. It represents the four children of the sea god Lír who were turned into swans for 900 years by their jealous stepmother, leaving them nothing but their human voice. However, their singing was so magical that it dispelled all sorrow and filled the hearers' souls with a deep sense of peace.

Below: Oisín Kelly's evocative statue of the *Children of Lír*

Specialist Gardens
The **National Botanic Gardens** (▶ 134–135) at Glasnevin are well worth the journey from the city centre to see magnificent landscaped gardens with spectacular herbaceous borders, plant displays, arboretums and Victorian curvilinear glasshouses containing palms and other tropical plants. True garden lovers shouldn't miss the private garden of **Helen Dillon** (45 Sandford Road, open daily 2–6, Mar, Jul and Aug, and Sun Apr–Jun and Sep), whose truly splendid garden behind a handsome Georgian terrace in the Southside suburb of Ranelagh is a magnet for visitors on sunny Sunday afternoons.

People &

No visitor can escape the presence of those legendary figures who shaped Dublin's history and whose devotion and patriotism shaped the course of the country's history. Their memory lives on everywhere in the city, in its place-names and its monuments.

Politics

St Patrick (5th century)

Christianity first came to Ireland around the beginning of the 5th century with the arrival of St Patrick, the patron saint of Ireland who, according to legend, rid the country of its snakes. He is said to have used the shamrock, with its leaf divided into three, to illustrate the oneness of the Holy Trinity. The shamrock, as a result, has become the national emblem of Ireland.

Celebrating St Patrick's Day
Below: Shamrock carving

Jonathan Swift (1667–1745)

Satirist, political journalist and churchman, Jonathan Swift was Dean of St Patrick's Cathedral from 1713 to 1745, during which time he became a fierce advocate for the economic rights of the Irish people. Many of his best-known works were written during this time, including his greatest satire, *Gulliver's Travels*, often regarded as a children's book, but in fact one of the most powerful exposés of human folly ever penned.

Theobald Wolfe Tone (1763–98)

This radical Protestant lawyer and "Father of Irish Republicanism" founded the United Irishmen in 1791, and staged illegal meetings in the Tailor's Hall (► 71). It is thought that their unsuccessful 1798 revolt helped to convince the British Government to impose the Act of Union and direct rule from London.

Arthur Guinness (1725–1803)

Arthur Guinness was just 34 when he acquired the small, disused Rainsford's Ale Brewery in St James's Gate in 1759 and started black-roasting malt to produce *Guinness* (➤ 57–60). Today, his legacy persists in the heady malt and hop smells that waft across Dublin, and in the 10 million glasses of *Guinness* consumed in more than 120 countries worldwide every day.

Daniel O'Connell (1775–1847)

Known as "the Liberator", Daniel O'Connell was a brilliant politician, lawyer and orator who secured Catholic emancipation for Ireland in 1829, rallying support

Countess Markievicz (1868–1927)

In 1908, Countess Constance Markievicz, a member of the Anglo-Irish landed gentry class, became committed to the nationalist cause and joined Sinn Féin (a national political party in Ireland). A key military figure in the 1916 Easter Rising (➤ 54), she escaped execution only on account of her public status and gender. In 1918 she became the first woman to be elected to the British House of Commons but, in keeping with Sinn Féin's policy, she refused to take her seat.

James Larkin (1876–1947)

Liverpool-born "Big Jim" Larkin, the great trade

Right: Irish republican leader, Eámon de Valera

James Larkin – workers' leader

through enormous, non-violent mass meetings. Sadly, his peaceful methods were not successful in gaining Home Rule for the Irish, but his achievements none the less earned him an eternal place in Dubliners' hearts and in Dublin's main street (➤ 126–127), now named after him.

THE SHAPING OF A NATION

Key figures in the 1916 Easter Rising included labour union organiser **James Connolly**; poet **Pádraic Pearse**, leader of Irish nationalism, who proclaimed Ireland's independence from Britain from the steps of the General Post Office (➤ 127); **Michael Collins**, head of the Irish Volunteers' campaign of urban guerrilla warfare; and **Eámon de Valera**, the motivator of the hardline Irish Republican Army (IRA). All were imprisoned at Kilmainham Gaol (➤ 54–56). De Valera went on to lead his country through its final severance with Britain in a 16-year term as Taoiseach (prime minister; pronounced T-shock), and in 1959 became president of Ireland. It must have been with mixed emotions that he opened the gaol as a museum in 1966.

unionist, changed the lives of thousands of unskilled labourers who, in early 20th-century Dublin, worked and lived in some of the worst conditions in Europe. Their employers feared Larkin so much that they ordered their workers to sign a declaration that they would not join his Irish Transport and General Workers Union. This led to the bitter "Dublin lock-out", which lasted from August 1913 to February 1914, during which time the city ground to a standstill, forcing a new era in industrial relations in the city and the country.

CÚ CHULAINN

A small bronze statue of Cú Chulainn – the greatest of all Irish mythical heroes – stands in the General Post Office (➤ 127) in memory of the participants of the 1916 Easter Rising. According to legend, when mortally wounded in battle, Cú tied himself to a pillar so that he might face his enemies even in death. Only when a raven perched on his shoulder did they dare to approach.

Mary Robinson (1944–)

Mary Robinson, a liberal lawyer and graduate of Trinity College, became the first woman president of the Republic of Ireland in December 1990. Her appointment was seen as a sign of more enlightened times, challenging the old paternalism of Irish politics. Seven years later she relinquished the presidency to take on an international role as United Nations High Commissioner for Human Rights.

An A–Z of Musica Dublin

ALTAN was one of the first groups to successfully put traditional music into a modern context in the folk revival of the 1960s and 1970s. They frequently performed in Dublin pubs.

The Dubliners in concert

The **BODHRÁN** (pronounced "boran"), a one-sided drum made from goatskin, is one of the country's most ancient instruments – a subtle and exciting instrument that stirs the Irish spirit when played.

The **COMMITMENTS** (1991), a film about a fictitious Dublin band based on the eponymous novel by Roddy Doyle (▶ 12), gripped the imagination of cinema-goers worldwide. Andrew Strong, the lead singer, went on to a successful solo musical career.

The **DUBLINERS** were among the first bands to launch Irish folk music on to the international stage. In the 1970s they frequently played in O'Donoghue's (▶ 116), a leading city music pub.

EMIGRATION following the 1845 potato famine paradoxically helped to preserve Irish music. Many new songs about the hardships of the time were composed and those fleeing Ireland spread Celtic music to foreign shores.

The **FIDDLE**, when combined with the flute and *uilléan* pipes, forms the essence of the Irish traditional sound.

In the 1960s the **GRESHAM HOTEL** was the birthplace of The Chieftains, Ireland's greatest exponents of traditional music, and the only live venue in Ireland of the Beatles, who held an impromptu session here.

The **HOTHOUSE FLOWERS** got their lucky break during the 1990s in Grafton Street, where they used to busk as the Bendini Brothers.

The **IRISH DANCE COMMISSION**, established in Dublin in 1931, led to the resurgence of *céilis*, lively organised occasions of set dancing central to Irish traditional music, and still popular today.

JIGS, REELS AND HORNPIPES form the three oldest, and most often heard, forms of Irish dance.

*"**KIND** friends and companions,*
together combine,
Come raise up your glasses in chorus
with mine.
We will drink and be merry, all grief to
refrain

Riverdance

That we may or might never all meet
here again."
– Anon, A traditional Irish song

LIVE AID, the mega-pop concert initiated and organised by Bob Geldof, lead singer of the Dublin band The Boomtown Rats, took the world by storm in 1985, raising more than $100 million for Ethiopia.

Handel's ***MESSIAH*** premièred in the Music Hall in Fishamble Street in 1742, performed by the joint choirs of St Patrick's and Christ Church cathedrals.

NOTHING COMPARES TO YOU was the title of Dublin-born Sinead O'Connor's greatest ever hit. Before becoming a star, she worked as a kissogram and as a waitress in the Bad Ass Café (► 76).

"OLD-STYLE SINGING" (called *sean-nós*) is the most likely type of traditional song you'll hear in a Dublin pub – simple, unaccompanied solo performances about love, immigration, politics, murders, drinking, lullabies and laments…

Uilléan **PIPES** have been the quintessential Irish instrument since the 1700s. In the hands of an accomplished player the sound can resemble an entire orchestra.

RIVERDANCE, with its theatrical spectacle and modern take on traditional dance forms, set the world alight with a passion for all things Irish.

SHARON, ANDREA, CAROLINE AND JIM – the Dublin-based family quartet who comprise The Corrs – continue to wow the world with their seductive blend of mellow American rock and traditional Irish music.

THIN LIZZY took the world by storm with "Celtic Rock" sounds. Before stardom, lead singer Phil Lynott busked under Merchant's Arch in Temple Bar.

U2 is today Ireland's greatest music export. Among the world's most successful rock bands, they continue to live, work and play in Dublin. In 2000, they were awarded the Freedom of the City.

VICAR STREET, together with Whelan's (► 82), is a top venue for up-and-coming local bands.

WESTLIFE is just one of the world-renowned pop groups to have emerged from the local music scene in the latest craze for boy- and girl-bands, together with Boyzone (with its teen-pop-idol Dublin-born former lead-singer Ronan Keating) and B*witched.

YOU will have to follow the city's music trail, the Rock 'n' Stroll Trail (► 167) for further details of Dublin's extraordinary musical legacy.

The traditional rivalry between the people of north and south Dublin is legendary. Divided geographically by the Liffey, Dublin, many would argue, is also divided economically and socially. The recent development of Temple Bar into a smart, trendy cultural quarter exacerbated the divide between north and south. But now, times are changing as the Northside experiences such new developments as the International Financial Services Centre in the smart, renovated docklands area and the reformation of Smithfield Market.

NORTHSIDE vs SOUTHSIDE

This new-found vitality north of the Liffey has put paid to many a Southsider's joke although, further afield, some of the tenement districts and housing estates of the northern outskirts still provide stark contrast to the affluent period residences and the graceful Georgian squares of the fashionable Southside.

Currently, *the* most fashionable address to have is Dublin 4 – Southside, of course, embracing the districts of Ballsbridge, Donnybrook and Sandycove. Leafy Ballsbridge is especially exclusive with its grand Georgian residences. It is also known as the Embassy District for the proliferation of foreign embassies that have established themselves here. Here, too, are such landmarks as the Lansdowne Road stadium, the home of the Irish national rugby team, and the Royal Dublin Society Showgrounds, host to the Dublin Horse Show (▶ 32).

Neighbouring Sandymount is famous for its seaside promenade, which runs all the way to Dun Laoghaire. (Don't

Above: The north bank of the Liffey

Top right: Bird's-eye view from The Chimney

Right: Georgian town houses grace the city

confuse it with the similar-sounding district of Sandycove further out.) Here the James Joyce Museum, housed in the Martello tower featured in his blockbusting *Ulysses*, is a must-see for fans of the writer.

DARTING ABOUT

The DART railway is the best way to explore the outlying districts of Dublin. It takes passengers speedily to various destinations and, for those heading south, it provides sensational coastal views as it curves along the fringes of Dublin Bay.

Dalkey: This attractive Southside seaside village of brightly painted villas was once called the "Town of Seven Castles", but only two of these fortified mansions remain. Just offshore, Dalkey Island can be visited by boat in summer.

Killiney: This salubrious Southside address is home to Formula One driver Damon Hill, U2's Bono and other celebrities. The bracing climb to the top of Killiney Hill (above) is rewarded with sensational coastal vistas high above popular, pebbly Killiney Strand.

Howth: This north Dublin seaside suburb and fishing port is one of the city's most sought-after addresses, bustling with top-notch fish restaurants, lively pubs and a large sailing fraternity. The promontory of Howth Head (► 164–166), overlooking Dublin Bay, is especially popular with walkers.

PADDY'S DAY

Throughout the world Irishmen and women join together to celebrate St Patrick's Day, but the biggest festivities are held in Dublin, where an exuberant four-day festival of contemporary and traditional music, song and dance culminates in a spectacular parade, all-night parties and flamboyant firework extravaganzas. Look out for Bono and St Patrick look-a-likes, human shamrocks, and a variety of other local characters in entertaining costumes. Traditionally, everyone wears a shamrock, Ireland's national emblem (► 23), but nowadays it seems that anything goes. Some years they even dye the Liffey green!

January

On the stroke of midnight on **New Year's Day** (1 January), Dubliners start the year the way they mean to continue it…partying!

The Dublin CALENDAR

Dubliners love having fun. As a result their social calendar is filled with *fleadh* (festivals; pronounced flah), sporting fixtures, religious occasions, cultural events and other good reasons to celebrate. Here are some of the highlights:

ULYSSES

James Joyce's most celebrated novel, *Ulysses*, modelled on Homer's *Odyssey*, takes the wanderings of the hero Ulysses and re-enacts them in the fictional hero Leopold Bloom, walking the streets of Dublin on a single day – 16 June, 1904. Much of Joyce's Dublin still exists and, on the same day every year, enthusiastic costumed Joyceans gather together to retrace Bloom's steps, starting from the tower in Sandycove where the novel opens – today it houses the James Joyce Museum (▶ 29). Real fanatics commence the route with a "Joyce breakfast" of kidneys and *Guinness*, and lunch, like Bloom, on a gorgonzola sandwich and a glass of burgundy at Davy Byrne's (▶ 112).

February

Anyone who's visited Dublin for a Rugby International weekend at Croke Park (Lansdowne Road is due to reopen in 2009) – is likely to have had an experience they will never forget. The **Six Nations Rugby Tournament** (varying Saturdays February to April) is one of the great social events of the year, with big crowds out to support the "Boys in Green" against England, Wales, Scotland, France and Italy.

March

If you could choose just one day to be in Ireland's capital city, it would have to be **St Patrick's Day** (17 March, ▶ opposite).

April

The **Colours Boat Race** (first weekend), a hugely competitive rowing race on the Liffey between Trinity College and UCD (University College Dublin), marks the first of several river-centred events in the Dublin calendar.

Also in April is the **Dublin Film Festival**, of international stature, screening old and classic movies at various cinemas throughout the city. Details from Dublin Tourism (▶ 37).

May

On 1 May, Dubliners need little excuse to party, celebrating this national holiday with showy **May Day** parades.

August

Staged at the Royal Dublin Society Showgrounds in Ballsbridge, the **Dublin Horse Show** (second week) is a premier social event as well as a sporting one. It is the highlight of the Irish equestrian year and a magnet for horse-lovers from all over the world, with show-jumping and dressage, and a chance to show off your hat on Ladies' Day.

June

16 June in Dublin is **Bloomsday**, a quirky day of literary commemoration based on the events in Ulysses (► 31). Fans of James Joyce enjoy readings, walking tours and re-enactments of scenes from his masterwork.

June also marks the start of **Music in the Park**, a summer series of lunchtime concerts in various city parks. Details from Dublin Tourism (► 37).

July

Summer festivities in **Temple Bar** (► 68–69) peak with the **Temple Bar Blues Fleadh** (third weekend) – three days of live blues music featuring international stars.

TRADITIONAL IRISH SPORTS

There's nothing like spending a Sunday at **Croke Park** (► 135), where the Irish cheer for their county in full voice for a championship game of Gaelic football (below) or a hurling match. Hurling is the Irish national game and one of the fastest and most exciting field games in the world. It's akin to hockey, but in hurling the ball can be carried on the flat end of the stick (hurley) and it can be hit in the air. Its origins can be dated back to pre-Christian history and legend. The Irish mythological hero and warrior Cú Chulainn (► 25) is said to have won a match single-handedly against 150 opponents!

September

Since 1920, Dubliners have enjoyed watching swimmers as they brave the murky waters of the River Liffey from Rory O'More Bridge to the Custom House in the **Liffey Swim** (first Saturday).

Even bigger crowds turn out for the **All-Ireland Hurling Final** (second Sunday) and the **All-Ireland Gaelic Football Final** (fourth Sunday), two of the country's main sporting events, both played at Croke Park to sell-out crowds (▶ opposite).

EQUESTRIAN PRIDE

Horse-racing has been popular in Ireland for centuries – it was here that the term "steeple-chasing" emerged, with an epic cross-country race from one church to another. Owners, breeders and trainers worldwide have long favoured Irish bloodstock, and Irish jockeys are always in big demand. In Dublin, the country's pride in the sporting horse can be enjoyed at the many race meetings at Leopardstown Park (tel: 01 289 3607), at the celebrated Dublin Horse Show (above and opposite), or by visiting the **National Stud** southwest of Dublin at Tully in the "Thoroughbred County" – County Kildare (tel: 045 521617, open mid-Feb to mid-Nov, 9:30–6).

October

This is a busy month culturally, with the **Dublin Theatre Festival** (first two weeks) and the **Guinness Jazz Festival** (final weekend), Ireland's largest and longest-running jazz festival.

The main celebration, **Samhain** (Hallowe'en, 31 October) is one of Dublin's few genuinely Celtic traditions, with a spectacular night-time parade of witches, druids, monsters, devils, ghouls and fire-breathing dragons.

December

December means **Pantomime Season** and **Christmas** (25 December), with Christian celebrations involving going to midnight mass on Christmas Eve.

On **St Stephen's Day** (26 December), Catholic boys dress up as chimney sweeps with blackened faces and sing hymns to raise money for charity.

The **Leopardstown Races** (26–29 December), one of the main events in Dublin's prestigious horse-racing calendar, are always a splendid affair of colour, noise, drama and excitement.

Only The Very Best Now...

Best bird's-eye viewpoints
- Guinness Storehouse (➤ 57–60)
- Smithfield Chimney (➤ 128)

Best pubs for traditional Irish entertainment
- Abbey Tavern, Howth (➤ 140)
- Johnnie Fox's, Glencullen (➤ 145)
- Keating's, D1 (➤ 140)
- Oliver St John Gogarty, D2 (➤ 78 and 81)
- O'Donoghue's, D2 (➤ 116)
- O'Shea's Merchant, D8 (➤ 82)
- Slattery's, D1 (➤ 140)

Best sculptures
- *Children of Lir*, Garden of Remembrance, Parnell Square (➤ 22)
- *Famine Figures*, Custom House Quay (➤ 158)
- *James Joyce*, Earl Street North (➤ 13)
- *Jim Larkin*, O'Connell Street (➤ 127)
- *Molly Malone*, Grafton Street Lower (➤ 105)
- *Oscar Wilde*, Merrion Square (➤ 106–107)
- *Patrick Kavanagh* – beside the Grand Canal (near Baggot Street Bridge)
- *Spire of Dublin*, O'Connell Street (➤ 127)

Above: Statue of *Molly Malone*

Best for kids
- Dublinia (➤ 71)
- GAA Museum, Croke Park (➤ 135)
- National Wax Museum (➤ 129)
- Temple Bar (➤ 68–69)
- Dublin Zoo (➤ 124)

Opposite: Taking a break outside the Bank of Ireland

Best buys
- Irish designer fashions – at the Design Centre (➤ 79)
- Jewellery – at Designyard (➤ 80) or the National Museum Shop (➤ 115)
- Books – at Greene's (➤ 115)
- Whiskey – tax free at the airport
- Waterford Glass – at House of Ireland (➤ 114)
- Knitware – at Kilkenny Shop (➤ 114)
- Linen – at the Kilkenny Shop (➤ 114) or Duck Lane (➤ 138)
- Handicrafts and gifts – at Avoca Handweavers (➤ 114)
- Cheese – at Sheridan's Cheesemongers (➤ 115)

If you only go to one...
Attraction: The *Book of Kells*, Trinity College (➤ 91–92)
Pub: Mulligan's (➤ 113)
Hotel: The Shelbourne (➤ 42 and 111–112), if only for afternoon tea
Bar: The Gravity Bar, Guinness Storehouse (➤ 60)
Shop: Brown Thomas (➤ 114)
City walking tour: Pub Crawl (➤ 159–161)

Finding Your Feet

First Two Hours

Dublin is well served by its international airport, two ferry ports and two railway stations. Both ports and the airport have foreign exchange bureaux, the major car-rental firms, bus transfers to the city centre and taxi ranks.

Arriving By Air

- Dublin Airport is **12km (8 miles) north of the city centre**. There is only one terminal with Departures on the upper level and Arrivals on the lower level.
- To get to **Dublin city centre by car**, take the M1 south and follow signs. The journey takes between 20 minutes and an hour depending on traffic.
- **Taxis** are always metered and a journey to the city centre should be relatively inexpensive. The taxi rank is on the Arrivals level. Be prepared to wait.
- To get to **Dublin city centre by bus**, there are several options. Airlink bus No 747 leaves every 15 minutes from Arrivals to O'Connell Street, Busáras (the central bus terminal) and Parnell Square. Airlink bus No 748 will also take you to Tara Street, Aston Quay and Heuston Station. For further information contact Dublin Bus (tel: 01 873 4222; www.dublinbus.ie). Tickets are available at the CIE Information Desk in Arrivals.
- If you plan to use the bus regularly in the city centre, consider buying one of the special **Rambler bus passes** (➤ opposite).
- The **Aircoach express service** operates 5am–midnight from Arrivals, with departures every 15 minutes. City-centre stops include O'Connell Street, Grafton Street, Merrion Square North, Pembroke Road and St Stephen's Green. Tickets are available from the Tourist Information desk in Arrivals. For further information contact Aircoach (tel: 01 844 7118; www.aircoach.ie).
- The **cheapest way into the city** is by public bus (Nos 16A, 41, 41A, 41B and 41C); buses operate every 10–20 minutes from the airport to Eden Quay, near O'Connell Street. These are slower than the Airlink and Aircoach services with numerous stops *en route*.

Arriving By Boat

- **Ferries from the UK** sail into the ports of Dublin, 5km (3 miles) east of the city, and Dun Laoghaire (pronounced "Dunleary"), 14km (9 miles) south of the city.
- If **travelling by car** to Dublin, simply follow city-centre signs.
- **Taxis and coaches** operate from both ports into the centre of Dublin.
- **Public buses** run regularly to the centre: catch No 7, 7A, 46A or 46X from Dun Laoghaire DART Station; Nos 53 or 53A from Dublin Port. A special Dublin Bus shuttles between the ferry terminal and Busáras (the central bus station) every half-hour 7am–11:10pm daily. The journey takes around ten minutes.
- **An inexpensive DART service** (➤ 38) from Dun Laoghaire to Dublin runs every half-hour (sometimes more frequently) to Pearse, Tara Street and Connolly stations in the city centre. The journey takes 25 minutes.

Arriving By Train

- Dublin has **two mainline stations**. Passengers from the north arrive at Connolly Station, while trains from the south and west operate in and out of Heuston Station. Buses and taxis are available at both stations.
- **For rail information**, contact Irish Rail/Iarnród Éireann (tel: 01 836 6222; www.irishrail.ie).

Tourist Information Offices

- The **main Dublin tourist office** is located inside a converted church in Suffolk Street. It helps with reservations and information on what's on.
- **Dublin Tourism**, Suffolk Street, Dublin 2 (tel: 1850 23 03 30, information; 1800 66 86 68, reservations; www.visitdublin.com; open Jul–Aug Mon–Sat 9–7, Sun 10:30–3; Sep–Jun Mon–Sat 9–5:30).
  Several other tourist information offices are placed at strategic spots around the city: **Dun Laoghaire Ferry Terminal** (open Mon–Sat 10–1, 2–6); **Dublin Airport Arrivals Hall** (open daily 8am–10pm); **14 O'Connell Street**, opposite the Dublin Bus offices (open Mon–Sat 9–5); **Baggot Street Bridge** (open Mon–Fri 9:30–noon, 12:30–5).
- The website of the **Irish Tourist Board** (www.ireland.ie) is useful for information on Ireland in general.
- The **Dublin Pass** gives free entry to more than 30 attractions and other offers, including transport to and from Dublin airport. It is available as a 1-, 2-, 3- or 6-day pass.

Getting Around

The city is divided into two halves by the River Liffey, which neatly bisects it from east to west. These two areas are popularly referred to as Northside and Southside.

Public Transport

Buses are the main form of public transport in the city, with the DART (Dublin Area Rapid Transit) train system and the new LUAS tramway being the most popular ways to reach the suburbs. (See the transport map on the inside back cover for all routes.)

Bus

- **Dublin Bus** operates a **comprehensive network** of bus routes throughout the city and into the suburbs, Mon–Sat 6am–11:30pm, Sun 10am–11:30pm, and a **Nitelink limited service** on selected routes Mon–Sat after midnight. For route details, contact Dublin Bus (tel: 01 873 4222; www.dublinbus.ie).
  The **number** and **destination** (in English and Irish) are displayed on the front of each bus. *An Lar* means city centre.
- **Tickets** can be bought on the bus (no change given). **Timetables** and **prepaid tickets** can be bought from the Dublin Bus desk at the airport, the main ticket office (59 O'Connell Street Upper; open Mon–Fri 9–5:30, Sat 9–2) or at any of the 300 Dublin Bus ticket agents around the city.
- Consider purchasing a 1-, 3- or 5-day **Rambler Ticket**. These special passes offer unlimited travel for consecutive days on all Dublin Bus scheduled services, including the Airlink express coach service (► 36), excluding Nitelink and special tours.
- The **Family Ticket** is valid for use by a family not exceeding two adults and four children under 16 years, for unlimited travel for one day only on all Dublin Bus scheduled services (except Nitelink and special tours).
- If you plan to explore County Dublin, consider an **Adult Short Hop pass**, valid for unlimited travel for one day for one adult on all Dublin Bus, DART and Suburban Rail scheduled services; a **Family Short Hop day**

pass valid for an immediate family (not exceeding two adults and four children under 16 years).

- Special **student passes** are available on production of a current ISIC Card.
- All tickets must be inserted into the **ticket validator** on the right-hand side as you enter the bus.

DART

- The **DART** (Dublin Area Rapid Transit) is a **light rail service**, operated by Irish Rail, serving 28 stations from Malahide in the north to Greystones in the south.
- Main city-centre stations are **Connolly** (north of the river), and **Tara Street** and **Pearse** (both south of the river).
- **Trains run** every five minutes in rush hours, every 10–15 minutes at other times of the day Mon–Sat 6:30am–midnight and less frequently Sun 9:30am–11pm.
- **Single tickets** are available from any DART station, but it can be cheaper to buy a one-day unlimited DART travel ticket or a family pass. Validating machines, where provided, must be used.
- Irish Rail sells **a range of combined travel passes** in conjunction with Dublin Bus (► 37) and the LUAS tramway.

LUAS

- A new **tramway** system opened in summer 2004. At present it has only two routes (organised into three zones) to the suburbs and is primarily used by commuters.
- LUAS offers a range of ticket options from a single trip to a 30-day pass, together with 1-, 7- and 30-day **Combi-tickets** for LUAS and Dublin Bus.

Taxi

- There are **plenty of taxis** in Dublin, but on Friday and Saturday nights you may have to wait for a short while.
- Taxis are found at **taxi ranks** or can be **hailed on the street**.

Car

- Traffic in Ireland **drives on the left**.
- Drivers and all passengers **must wear seat belts**.
- **The speed** limit is 48kph (30mph) in towns, 96kph (60mph) on other roads and 112kph (70mph) on motorways.
- The **legal alcohol limit** is 80mg alcohol per 100ml blood (8 percent).
- The volume of traffic in Dublin is increasing and **parking is expensive** and limited.
- **Try to avoid** weekday morning and late-afternoon rush hours (7:30–8/9am and 4–6pm), keep out of bus lanes and use car-parks.
- The **North and South Circular roads** circumscribe the core of Dublin, and most of the city's sights are located within this area. The city's main thoroughfare is **O'Connell Street**. The quays alongside the Liffey are one-way: the south bank flows east to west and the north bank west to east.
- **Traffic wardens** take their job seriously and tow-away trucks are plentiful.
- Always **lock your car** and keep belongings out of sight.
- Some hotels and guest-houses have **private parking** for guests.

Car Hire

- All the main **car-rental companies** have desks in the Arrivals Hall at Dublin airport and in the city centre. Contact **Argus** (tel: 01 844 4257), **Budget** (tel: 01 844 5919), **Murrays Europcar** (tel: 01 812 0410) or **Hertz** (tel: 01 844 5466) for details.
- Hertz also has a desk at **Dun Laoghaire Harbour** (tel: 01 230 1769).

Postal Codes

Dublin is divided into 24 postal codes with unevenly numbered districts north of the Liffey and even ones to the south. The central areas – where you will probably spend most of your time – are D1 and D2.

D1 the main hub of the north bank.
D2 the heart of the south bank, including the main shopping district, Temple Bar, Trinity College and many of the key city sights.
D4 south and southeast of D2; this is one of Dublin's smartest districts, boasting some of its finest Georgian architecture.
D7 the western end of Northside, including Smithfield and Phoenix Park.
D8 the western end of Southside, including much of Viking and medieval Dublin, the two cathedrals and the Guinness factory.

Admission Charges

The cost of admission for museums, galleries and other places of interest mentioned in the book is indicated by the following price categories in Euros (€).

Inexpensive under €4   **Moderate** €4–6.50   **Expensive** over €6.50

Accommodation

Dublin is divided economically as well as geographically by the River Liffey, with the north inner-city tending to provide cheaper accommodation than the south side. This guide recommends a carefully selected cross-section of places to stay, ranging from luxury hotels to simple bed-and-breakfast accommodation.

- The most **exclusive hotels**, including the Merrion, the Shelbourne, the Clarence and the Fitzwilliam, offer top-notch world-class facilities with prices to match. These are all well located in the heart of town.
- You will also find many attractive **Georgian town houses**, which have been stylishly converted into small hotels and guest-houses, offering modern comforts in graceful surroundings while at the same time providing a glimpse of Dublin's glorious past.
- **Further out**, the tariffs will be lower and the buildings more recent (probably Victorian or Edwardian), but be prepared for a short bus or taxi ride into the city centre.
- **If you have a car**, think about staying even further out in the more peaceful suburbs, or on the coast at Portmarnock (➤ 42).
- If you are on a **tight budget** and want to **stay centrally**, consider a **hostel**. You may have to share facilities, but an increasing number now have private rooms. Among the best are **Isaacs** (2–5 Frenchmans Lane, tel: 01 855 6215), one of the longest-established, best-known hostels, in a converted wine warehouse north of the river near the central bus station; **Ashfield House** (19 D'Olier Street, tel: 01 679 7734), previously a church, now with clean, spacious twin rooms; and **Barnacles** (19 Temple Lane, tel: 01 671 6277), hugely popular and situated right at the heart of Dublin's trendy Temple Bar area.

Booking Accommodation

- All-year pressure on accommodation in Dublin has made it very expensive and it's advisable to **book well in advance**.
- Hotel rates quoted below **include service charges and VAT**. Prices can double during peak periods and some hotels offer reduced rates for quieter periods and weekends.
- Dublin Tourism offers an **on-the-spot booking service** for hostels, B&Bs, hotels, guest-houses and self-catering premises (tel: 1800 66 86 68 for reservations). You pay a standard booking fee and a 10 per cent deposit to Dublin Tourism (payable by credit card only), and the balance on arrival at your chosen accommodation.
- Reservations can also be made **on-line** through the Irish Tourist Board website (www.ireland.travel.ie).

Accommodation prices

Prices are per person sharing a double room per night

€ under €100   €€ €100–200   €€€ over €200

Aberdeen Lodge €

This charming private hotel in an elegant, restored Edwardian house combines century-old style with modern comforts, friendly service, a large garden and great food – including award-winning breakfasts. Set in an attractive tree-lined avenue in the quiet residential Southside suburb of Ballsbridge (➤ 28), conveniently located near the car ferry terminals and just five minutes' walk from the Sydney Parade DART Station, it makes a perfect base for exploring both the city centre and the Wicklow Mountains.

🚇 186 off C1   ✉ 53 Park Avenue, D4
☎ 01 283 8155; fax: 01 283 7877;
www.halpinsprivatehotels.com

Clarence €€€

This swish, minimalist, boutique hotel in Temple Bar is the trendiest address in town – a converted 19th-century Customs House on the banks of the Liffey owned by U2 band members Bono and The Edge. It offers all the luxuries and amenities expected by the many celebrities who stay here, with astonishing attention to detail. Treat yourself to a night in the multi-level penthouse suite. At a cost of €2,100 per night, with an outdoor hot tub overlooking the river, this is surely Dublin's ultimate extravagance.

🚇 184 C4   ✉ 6–8 Wellington Quay, D2
☎ 01 407 0800; fax: 01 407 0820;
www.theclarence.ie

Clarion Hotel IFSC €€–€€€

Built with the business visitor in mind – it's right in the centre of the International Financial Services Centre – this high-rise, modern hotel has been a surprising hit with tourists. The rooms are big, bright and cheery and ideal for families. Ask for one at the front so you can enjoy the great views out over the mouth of the Liffey. Because it caters mostly to business travellers weekend bargains are often on offer.

🚇 185 F5   ✉ IFSC, D1   ☎ 01 433
8800; fax: 01433 8811;
www.clarionhotelifsc.com

Fitzwilliam €€€

You couldn't wish for a finer or more central location than that of the Fitzwilliam. Near Grafton Street (➤ 105) and overlooking St Stephen's Green (➤ 100–103), this hotel oozes modern comforts, impeccable service and understated luxury. Its striking interiors, created by English designer Terence Conran, give way to a new design concept entitled "Baronial Modern" – a tarkly modern interpretation of features typical of a country house, with frosted glass, leather sofas, angular surfaces, moody down-lighting and accents of cream, purple and chrome. Top-floor front rooms have balconies with breathtaking bird's-eye views of the Green; others overlook the country's largest roof garden. One of Ireland's top chefs, Kevin Thornton, has his highly acclaimed eponymous restaurant here (▶ 112).

➕ 184 C3 ✉ St Stephen's Green, D2
☎ 01 478 7000; fax: 01 478 7878;
www.fitzwilliam-hotel.com

Harding €

This bright, cheerful and surprisingly stylish hotel proves you can still be comfortable on a budget. Most of the 53 rooms here sleep three and all have private bathrooms. Situated at the heart of historic Dublin (the city's oldest street, Copper Alley, actually runs through the reception area), it is conveniently near Temple Bar, Dublin Castle, Christ Church cathedral and the Guinness Storehouse.

➕ 184 B4 ✉ Copper Alley,
Fishamble Street, D2 ☎ 01 679
6500; fax: 01 679 6504;
www.hardinghotel.ie

Lansdowne Hotel €–€€

This small, friendly hotel in a converted Georgian house in the stylish suburb of Ballsbridge combines homely, pleasant facilities with a popular bar and a Celtic-themed restaurant serving fine Irish cuisine, all just a stone's throw from Lansdowne Road rugby stadium and the Royal Dublin Showgrounds.

➕ 186 B1 ✉ 29 Pembroke Road, D4
☎ 01 668 2522; fax: 668 5585;
www.lansdownehotel.com

Longfields €–€€

Centrally located near Merrion Square and St Stephen's Green, in the midst of the Georgian quarter, this charming, small hotel with its personal service, period furnishings and intimate award-winning restaurant, Longechamp at No 10, makes a perfect retreat after a busy day's shopping and sightseeing.

➕ 185 E2 ✉ 9–10 Fitzwilliam Street
Lower, D2 ☎ 01 676 1367;
fax: 01 676 1542; www.longfields.ie

Merrion €€€

Dublin's most luxurious five-star hotel consists of four gracious Grade I-listed Georgian town houses, sensitively restored to combine period elegance with top-class modern facilities. The magnificent 18th-century-style formal landscaped gardens help to create a peaceful retreat near the city centre. The hotel is connected to the eponymous restaurant of the celebrated Irish chef, Patrick Guilbaud (▶ 111).

➕ 185 E3 ✉ Merrion Street Upper,
D2 ☎ 01 603 0600; fax: 01 603 0700;
www.merrionhotel.com

Mont Clare €€

This is a large, friendly hotel with an attractive Georgian façade and well-equipped rooms offering excellent value for money in a fantastic city-centre location just round the corner from Trinity College, the National Gallery and the main shopping areas. There's even a lively traditional pub on the ground floor.

➕ 185 E3 ✉ Merrion Square, D2
☎ 01 607 3800; fax: 01 661 5663;
www.ocallaghanhotels.com

Morgan Hotel €€

Hidden amid the boutiques and pubs of the vibrant Temple Bar area, this new boutique hotel offers luxury city-centre accommodation at an affordable price. The 61 rooms are minimalist and chic, with great emphasis on aesthetic detail. They are also equipped with high-tech efficiency to suit the most discerning professional or leisure traveller, including video and CD players, and telephones with modems. Apart from the check-in area, there are no reception rooms, and breakfast is served in your room, but this somehow adds to the sense of exclusivity and seclusion.

➕ 185 D4 ✉ 10 Fleet Street, Temple Bar, D2 ☎ 01 679 3939; fax: 01 679 3946; www.themorgan.com

Morrison €€€

Superbly located on the north bank of the Liffey, the Morrison is a marvel of modern design. Ireland's top designer, John Rocha, had the last word on everything from toilets to staff uniforms. It is unabashedly smart, modern and sumptuous – a unique minimalist juxtaposition of wood, stone, steel and velvet – providing an exotic, serene haven far removed from the madness of the city centre on the doorstep. Its Halo restaurant (➤ 136–137) and bars are currently among the in-places to see and be seen.

➕ 184 C4 ✉ Ormond Quay Lower, D1 ☎ 01 887 2400; fax: 01 878 3185; www.morrisonhotel.ie

Number 31 €–€€

This award-winning B&B in the heart of Georgian Dublin is just a few minutes from St Stephen's Green. The former home of Sam Stephenson, Ireland's leading architect, it offers a variety of rooms spread over two striking buildings – a coach-house and a handsome town house – overlooking Fitzwilliam Place. Guests are encouraged to make themselves at home at any time of day.

➕ 185 E2 ✉ 31 Leeson Close, D2 ☎ 01 676 5011; fax: 01 676 2929; www.number31.ie

Raglan Lodge €

Guests always receive a warm welcome at this magnificent Victorian residence in a peaceful, leafy location just a ten-minute walk from the city centre. Each luxurious bedroom has all the necessary amenities for a high level of comfort, and the breakfasts are sensational.

➕ 186 A1 ✉ 10 Raglan Road, Dublin 4 ☎ 01 660 6697; fax: 01 660 6781

The Schoolhouse Hotel €€

This intimate and unusual hotel, housed in a former schoolhouse in trendy Ballsbridge, exudes a warm, friendly atmosphere. The superbly appointed bedrooms combine old-world charm with modern conveniences. The Schoolhouse ha retained many original features from its days as a school, and its former classrooms now house "The Canteen" restaurant and the lively Schoolhouse bar. It is gaining a reputation for quality modern Irish cuisine in an unusual setting.

➕ 186 A2 ✉ 2–3 Northumberland Road, D4 ☎ 01 667 5014; fax: 01 667 5015; www.schoolhousehotel.com

The Shelbourne Hotel €€€

The renovated Shelbourne (➤ 111–112) has been rated Dublin's most distinguished hotel, hosting the royal and the famous ever since its opening in the 18th century. Authors as diverse as Thackeray and Elizabeth Bowen have sung its praises in their work. In 1921, it was the setting for the signing of the Irish constitution. Today, with its luxurious rooms, two bars, two restaurants, spa and health centre, it ranks among the greatest hotels of the world – opulent and extravagant, yet surprisingly personal.

➕ 185 D3 ✉ 27 St Stephen's Green, D2 ☎ 01 663 4500; fax: 01 661 6006; www.shelbourne.ie

Further Afield
Portmarnock Hotel & Golf Links €€–€€€

A luxurious seaside hotel in the former home of the famous Jameson whiskey family, with an award-winning restaurant, spa and an 18-hole golf course designed by Bernhard Langer. Just 20 minutes from the city centre, it is ideally placed for visiting Malahide (➤ 147), Howth (➤ 164) and north County Dublin.

➕ 181 off F4 ✉ Portmarnock, County Dublin ☎ 01 846 0611; fax: 01 846 2442; www.portmarnock.com

Food and Drink

Eating out in Dublin has never been better. Restaurants and pubs have been opening with bewildering speed throughout the city over the past few years. A host of talented, young Irish chefs have appeared on the scene, and there is a noticeable emphasis on good-quality, local ingredients. What's more, there is an abundance of choice.

Many of the most favoured eateries can be found around Temple Bar and in the busy network of streets between Dawson Street and South Great George's Street, but some of the real culinary gems have to be sought out further afield in the lesser-known back streets and suburbs. Whether you're after a gourmet feast, a stylish meal somewhere chic, a cheap-and-cheerful snack, or wholesome, hearty pub food, one thing's for sure – eating out in Dublin combines genuine hospitality, high standards and really good value for money.

International Cooking

- Changes in **food fashions** have resulted in dramatic developments on the restaurant front recently, with the emergence of numerous trendy, minimalist *nouveau* eateries with strong emphasis on global cuisine. Mediterranean, Tex-Mex, Asian fusion, Indian, Italian…all the main cuisines are well represented, with Thai and Japanese restaurants making a particular impact.
- This diversity is relatively new to Ireland and is something which local chefs have seized upon with great enthusiasm. As a result, many of these vibrant, new restaurants offer truly **"international" cuisine**, with an astonishing range of ingredients and flavours from all over the world, combined in irresistible, innovative ways.

Irish Cooking

- Alongside foreign cuisine, Irish cooking has made a comeback. Several of the city's top chefs are working on the concept of a **New Irish Cuisine** – light, modern interpretations of traditional dishes and ingredients (► 18–19).
- At the other end of the scale, simple, nourishing portions of **traditional Irish fare** (► 16–18) remain the order of the day in some restaurants, although they are usually easier to find in pubs.
- For many visitors, the **pub atmosphere** is especially enjoyable, and it is often a good choice, enabling you to savour a glass of *Guinness* or any of the excellent Irish-brewed beers with your meal.

Pubs

- Dublin's pubs exist for **drinking not dining**, but an increasing number are providing excellent fare at lunchtime and some offer meals into the early evening too. Many will serve coffee at any time of day, including Irish coffees – a delicious concoction of coffee, cream and whiskey.
- For decades, all the **city pubs** were similar in style – smoky, intimate, reliable and full of locals and old timers. Then, as Dublin began to flourish, glitzy, new-wave, lounge-style bars, trendy mega-pubs and theme bars (which locals disparagingly call "Euro-swiggers") began to open, drawing a young and lively crowd, and pandering to the huge numbers of stag- and hen-night celebrants who descend on the Irish capital at weekends.

- Along with the city's great icon drink of *Guinness*, some pubs are now serving exciting **new stouts and ales** made by Ireland's creative new micro-breweries.
- Even though the city is changing fast, the pub remains at the very **hub of its social life**, and with more than a thousand different pubs listed in the Dublin phone book, there are watering-holes to suit all tastes and ages.

Cafés

- Together with the arrival of an exciting new café society, Dublin has gone crazy over **coffee** in the past few years. New names such as Insomnia and The Joy of Coffee are springing up throughout the city alongside old favourites such as Butler's Chocolate Café (➤ 76) and the Avoca Café (➤ 109).
- Cafés also prove a popular choice for **lunch**, with many of the most attractive ones located in museums or shopping centres – such as Dublin City Gallery The Hugh Lane (➤ 130), Kilkenny Shop (➤ 114), Dublin Writers' Museum (➤ 131) and the Powerscourt Townhouse (➤ 74).

Practical Tips

- **Booking** is essential for most restaurants, particularly at weekends.
- **Lunch is usually served** between noon and 2:30 and dinner between 6 and 11.
- Some of the top restaurants offer **excellent value fixed-price** lunch menus, making elegant dining surprisingly affordable. Many restaurants also have "early bird" deals, usually served around 6–7:30pm.
- **Most pubs open** Mon–Thu 10am–11:30pm, Fri–Sat 10am–12:30am, Sun noon–11pm. Also on Sunday, a few of the more traditional pubs observe "holy hour" and close their doors from 2–4pm, although if you are already inside you can usually stay and continue to drink.
- Many of the large pubs and music venues, generally described as **"late bars"**, have extended licences at the weekend and serve until 2am.
- A **service charge** of 12.5 per cent is generally added to the bill to tables of six or more in restaurants. If it's left to the customer, 10–15 per cent is the norm.
- A **smoking ban** in all public places (bars, restaurants, offices, etc.) has been in operation since 2004.
- **Dress code** is generally relaxed; few restaurants insist on jacket and tie.
- **Menus** are written in English.

Best traditional Irish cuisine
- Winding Stair (➤ 137)
- Ely (➤ 110)
- Gallagher's Boxty House (➤ 77)
- Old Jameson Distillery (➤ 129 and 137)
- Kilkenny (➤ 111)
- Oliver St John Gogarty (➤ 78)

Best coffee and cakes
- Avoca Café (➤ 109)
- The Shelbourne Hotel (➤ 42 and 111–112)

Best for beer
- Mulligan's (➤ 113)
- Grogan's (➤ 78)
- The Porterhouse (➤ 78)
- The Gravediggers (➤ 137)

Shopping

Ireland's capital is becoming increasingly fashionable as it rides its wave of prosperity and new-found confidence. Its image as a city of souvenir shops stuffed with lucky leprechauns and Celtic kitsch has faded as talented home-grown designers and craftsmen give the country's traditional elements of wood, silver, linen and wool a new twist. But what really sets Dublin apart from many other major cities is the wonderful mix of shopping available, making it a shopping tourist attraction in its own right.

- The bustling **city centre** provides the ideal setting for shopping, with some 3,000 shops and boutiques, many of which are still family owned.
- It's easy to walk around the main shopping areas in a day without the need for public transport and the creation of **pedestrian zones** in two distinct areas of the city has made shopping a particularly enjoyable experience.
- The **two main thoroughfares** – Henry Street (on the north side) with its high-street chain stores and good-value department shops, and Grafton Street (on the south side) with its chic boutiques – are both pedestrianised and are thriving as a result.
- The maze of streets around **Grafton Street** contains an intriguing mix of ultra-hip boutiques, old-fashioned stores and tiny off-beat shops making shopping here a delight.
- **Temple Bar** is a popular area for souvenirs, off-centre kitsch and trendy urban wear.
- The abundant **local specialities and crafts** make unique souvenirs. They range from delicate handmade jewellery, based on ancient Celtic designs, to hand-thrown ceramics and traditional musical instruments, while food and drink will keep the distinctive tastes of Dublin fresh long after your return home.

Antiques & Art

- **Antiques** can still be a good buy in Dublin, especially Georgian Irish furniture and silver (look for the harp in the hallmark), and early 20th-century Irish art has attracted worldwide acclaim.
- There are many commercial **art galleries** around the city. You can find a comprehensive list of them in the *Dublin Gallery Guide* (published by the Irish Contemporary Art Gallery Association) or in the free *In Dublin* listings magazine (▶ 48), published every other week.
- The **main shopping area** for antiques in the city is around Francis Street (▶ 80), and it's worth checking out the newspapers for local **auctions** too.

Books

Book-lovers will find that the literary capital of Europe won't disappoint. It is easy to while away an afternoon browsing in the the bookshop at the **Dublin Writers Museum** (▶ 131), or one of the city's countless other bookstores.

Fashion

There's no denying it, Dublin is chic! There are dozens of shops to appeal to all tastes from funky fashion outlets to big department stores, and the city has always had a great choice of antique, retro and second-hand clothing boutiques.

- As well as an abundance of foreign designer labels, local young design-ers have taken the **international fashion arena** by storm. Names to look out for include Lainey Keogh (knitwear); Louise Kennedy (suits); Philip Treacy (hats); Vivienne Walsh (jewellery); Orla Kiely (handbags), together with Quinn & Donnelly, Róisín Dubh, Aideen Bodkin, Marc O'Neill and Lyn Mar.
- You'll find **their work showcased** at Kilkenny (► 114), Brown Thomas (► 114), and the Design Centre (► 79).

Food & Drink

- **Traditional Irish foods** that travel well include smoked salmon (buy it vacuum packed), and some of the firmer, milder, handmade farmhouse cheeses such as Gubbeen and Durrus are also a good buy. They are widely available in delicatessens, specialist cheese shops and super-markets.
- The Irish are **famous for their drink**, so why not treat yourself to a bottle of Jamesons, Paddy or one of the numerous other Irish whiskeys on offer? Then there's Baileys (one of the world's top-selling drinks), Irish Mist (a sweet liqueur made from whiskey and honey), and *Guinness*, of course.

Glassware

- Irish **cut lead crystal** has been produced since the 18th century and is famous throughout the world. The best known is Waterford crystal, available in department stores and gift shops across the city.
- Look out for pieces by Irish designer **John Rocha**, who has been defining Irish fashions for more than a decade, and has now brought Waterford crystal back into vogue with his clean-cut, minimalist designs.

Handicrafts

- The shops along Nassau Street (► 113) sell some of Ireland's finest **handicrafts**. Look out for timeless tweeds, woollens, linen and lace, as well as delicate hand-cut jewellery, functional and arty ceramics and wrought ironware.
- **Knitwear** is highly popular and ranges from chunky Aran fishermen's sweaters to sophisticated fashion items, while **Irish linen** is world famous and hard-wearing – best buys include classic table- and bed-linen.

Music

- Dublin has an unusually large number of **record shops**.
- There are also several **specialist traditional and folk music outlets** selling instruments as well as CDs and cassettes.

Practical Tips

- **Opening hours** for most shops are Monday to Saturday, from 9 or 9:30am until 5:30 or 6pm. Some shops don't open until 10am; some close for lunch; others open on Sundays.
- Many **city-centre bookshops** keep longer hours, and some also open on Sunday afternoons.
- Thursday is **late-night shopping**, with the bigger stores and many of the smaller ones remaining open until about 8pm. Supermarkets tend to open late on Fridays.
- **Payment** can be made in Euros (€), Eurocheques or by credit cards. Some tourist shops accept sterling.
- Most high-street shops will **refund or exchange** goods as long as you keep your receipt and return the purchase within ten days.

Entertainment

Many people come to Dublin simply to have a good time, and they rarely leave disappointed. After all, it's not known as the European party capital for nothing! Going out in Dublin is a way of life. There's singing and dancing, clubs and drink. From cosy, old-fashioned watering-holes to smart designer bars and raucous theme pubs; from theatre to stand-up comedy; from traditional music to jazz; from classical to rock 'n' roll...there's something for everyone here, and it is this unique blend of the old with the new that attracts millions of visitors to Dublin from across the globe every year.

Pubs

- The quintessential **"Dublin pub"** (and there are more than a thousand to choose from) provides the focal point of many Dubliners' social life. It is here that conversation and *craic* (➤ 9) flows freely, creating that unique atmosphere that is the essence of Dublin and its friendly, sociable people.
- Many pubs, including O'Donoghue's (➤ 116), The Cobblestone (➤ 140), the Brazen Head (➤ 82) and O'Shea's Merchant (➤ 82 and 155), offer live **traditional Irish music**.

Live Music

- **Music and song**, whether classical, traditional or contemporary, play a large part as well, often experienced with its natural accompaniment – dance.
- The city provides a showcase for all tastes in music with numerous **live music venues** which, over the years, have given rise to such internationally renowned Irish folk musicians as The Dubliners and The Chieftains, and such pop artists as U2, Chris de Burgh, Boyzone and The Corrs.
- The most popular **late-night live music** venues for modern Irish and international acts include Vicar Street (➤ 82) and Whelan's (➤ 82).

Clubs

- Dublin is at the **cutting edge** of trendy pub and club culture, probably because of its youthful population. With 31 per cent of all Dubliners under 25, it is the youngest capital city in Europe.
- The most vibrant symbol of Dublin's nightlife is **Temple Bar** (➤ 68–69). An up-tempo enclave of restaurants and bars and a decidedly raucous "party animal" atmosphere, it draws a young and often rowdy crowd to its many clubs late at night.
- **Admission charges** to nightclubs vary; some are free. All clubs are pretty busy, especially at weekends.
- **Key city clubs** include Lillie's Bordello (➤ 116) and Spirit (➤ 140).

Theatre, Dance, Concerts & Cinema

- Dublin offers a **wonderful array** of dance, theatre, and classical and jazz concerts, ranging from world-class ballet at the National Concert Hall (➤ 115) and Riverdance at the The Point (➤ 140) to jovial local street musicians.
- The city's **theatre scene** continues to thrive with dozens of mainstream and fringe companies performing at such prestigious venues as the Abbey Theatre (➤ 139) and the Gate (➤ 139).

- Popular **Dublin-based dance troupes** include CoisCéim Dance Theatre and the Irish Modern Dance Theatre. Contact the Association of Professional Dancers (tel: 01 873 0288) for information on performance venues.
- **Opera Ireland** and the **Opera Theatre Company** perform regularly at a variety of city venues.
- **Comedy and cabaret** also feature strongly, staged at many pubs across the city including The International (► 160) on Wednesday nights, and the Ha'Penny Bridge Inn, 42 Wellington Quay, D2, on Tuesday and Thursday nights.
- Dubliners go to the cinema in greater numbers than any other city in Europe and there are numerous multiplexes and small cinemas throughout the city centre and suburbs. The Savoy on O'Connell Street and the little Screen cinema beside Trinity College are two old favourites.
- For theatre, concert and cinema details, look in a **listings magazine** or consult the local newspapers.

What's On When?

- Most **daily papers** include detailed listings of theatre, cinema, live music, sporting events and festivals. *The Irish Times* website (www.ireland.com) is also a valuable source of information.
- The free listings magazine, *In Dublin*, (published every two weeks) is available in some bars, hotels and attractions and contains information on theatre, cinema, museums, exhibitions, live music, nightclubs and restaurants, as well as the city's thriving gay scene.
- The free *Event Guide* can be found in most pubs, cafés, restaurants and record shops and provides a useful source of up-to-date information on all aspects of Dublin's nightlife, together with key events taking place throughout Ireland (www.eventguide.ie).
- *Hot Press* magazine is the bible of music and youth culture in Ireland, and contains handy listings on Dublin's contemporary music scene.

Tickets

- Tickets for many events are available on the night, but it is usually advisable to **book in advance**, especially for big-name artists, sporting events and such celebrated shows as Riverdance.

Sport

The Irish are passionate about sport, and Dubliners are no exception, so there is much to occupy the sports spectator here, including the very best in Gaelic football, hurling, international rugby, football and horse-racing events (► 31–33).

- For keen **golfers**, there are more than a hundred golf courses within 48km (30 miles) of Dublin, including the fabled fairways of the Royal Dublin, Bernhard Langer's Portmarnock Links, Druids Glen – voted European Golf Club of the Year 2000 – and The K Club, venue of the 2005 Ryder Cup. They all welcome visiting players. Contact the Golfing Union of Ireland (tel: 01 269 4111) for further information.
- **Hiking** is increasingly popular, with a mass exodus of Dubliners at weekends to the coast to Howth (► 164–166) and Bray Head, and to the Wicklow Mountains (► 144–145).
- The 136km (85-mile) **Wicklow Way**, one of Ireland's longest waymarked paths, starts in a southern suburb of Rathfarnham.

Southside West

Getting Your Bearings

The southwestern district is the least picturesque part of the city centre, but the most fascinating from an historic perspective. It includes a wealth of sights which, when pieced together, tell the story of Dublin from the very first Celtic settlers in AD 841 to the present day. It was here, according to legend, that St Patrick started converting the Irish to Christianity; where the Vikings created their small settlement of *Dubh Linn*; and where the medieval walled city of Dublin developed.

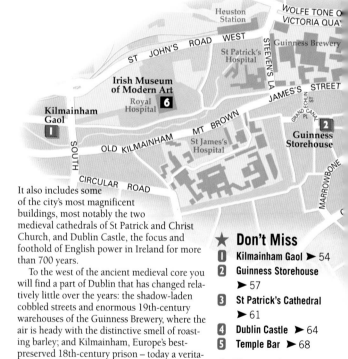

It also includes some of the city's most magnificent buildings, most notably the two medieval cathedrals of St Patrick and Christ Church, and Dublin Castle, the focus and foothold of English power in Ireland for more than 700 years.

To the west of the ancient medieval core you will find a part of Dublin that has changed relatively little over the years: the shadow-laden cobbled streets and enormous 19th-century warehouses of the Guinness Brewery, where the air is heady with the distinctive smell of roasting barley; and Kilmainham, Europe's best-preserved 18th-century prison – today a veritable shrine to those who suffered in the long and bitter struggle for Irish freedom.

In contrast, to the east, are the popular outdoor cafés and watering-holes of Temple Bar, once a derelict dockland area but now the most happening part of town and a hive of activity night and day.

★ Don't Miss

At Your Leisure

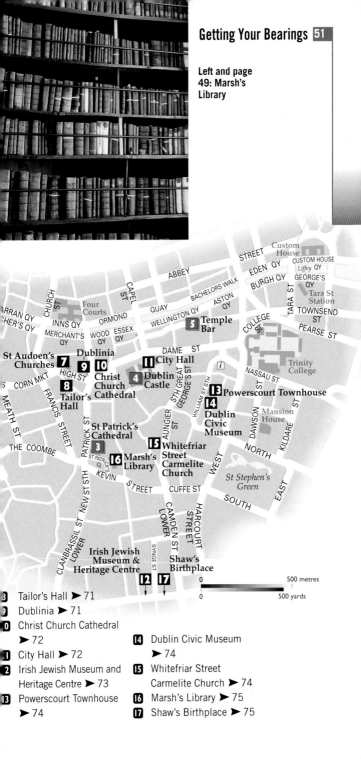

Left and page
49: Marsh's
Library

Southside West guarantees a full day's entertainment, from the gaol to the *Guinness* factory, and from the cathedrals and the Castle to a spot of shopping and some mighty good *craic*.

Southside West in a Day

9:30 am

Start at **1 Kilmainham Gaol** (right; ➤ 54–56), a grim, grey building steeped in Dublin's turbulent history. Not only does it provide an insight into what it was like to be confined in one of the forbidding cells, but it also documents some of the most heroic and tragic events in Ireland's emergence as a modern independent nation.

11:30 am

Hail a taxi and head eastwards to James's Gate, site of the massive Guinness Brewery – a 26ha (64-acre) sprawl of industry which churns out more than 10 million pints a day. Learn how it's produced at the state-of-the-art **2 Guinness Storehouse** (➤ 57–60).

1:00 pm

Spend your lunch break tucking into a hearty portion of Irish stew and sipping a perfect pint of the "black stuff" in one of three sky-high bars at the top of the Guinness Storehouse, while surveying the Brewery and the cityscape laid out seven storeys below.

2:00 pm

Trace the city's early history at either the medieval exhibitions of **9 Dublinia** (➤ 71) or **8 St Patrick's** (➤ 61–63), combined with a glance at the internal glories of **10 Christ Church Cathedral** (opposite, top; ➤ 72),

the city's first stone building, constructed in 1038. For a complete historical overview of the area's unique heritage, try the walking tour (▶ 152–154) and, if you have time, take a peek into the courtyard of **4 Dublin Castle** (▶ 64–67) – a mishmash of buildings of various periods which served as the headquarters of the British Administration until 1922 when it was handed over to the Irish Free State.

4:00 pm

There's just time to exercise your credit cards at the stylish Powerscourt House Shopping Centre, housed in a converted 18th-century mansion, or in the chic boutiques of the surrounding streets before the shops close at 6pm.

6:00 pm

Head to **5 Temple Bar** (▶ 68–69), Dublin's buzzing entertainment district and artistic quarter, where you're sure to find live music and great *craic* at its dozens of thriving restaurants, cafés, pubs and clubs (left). Temple Bar Market (below) takes place on Saturdays (▶ 80). Good traditional Dublin pubs? Try the Palace Bar on Fleet Street (▶ 81).

❶Kilmainham Gaol

On first impression, the dark, dank cells of an empty old prison may seem an unlikely place to visit. Yet Kilmainham Gaol provides a moving insight into some of the most profound and inspirational themes of modern Irish history. Many of the country's heroes were incarcerated here during the 140 years following the gaol's construction in 1787. Today it stands preserved as a powerful symbol of that long and bitter struggle for independence.

Historic moments

The chilling grey fortress of Kilmainham Gaol has frequently been compared to the Bastille in Paris. Indeed, its construction was inspired by the fear of French revolutionary ideals spreading to Ireland; a fear which ultimately found expression in the 1798 Rising. Before long the rebel leaders of the United Irishmen and the participants of the insurrection filled the cells. In 1803, following his abortive rebellion, Robert Emmet was imprisoned here together with 200 of his supporters. An heroic champion of Irish liberty, even the night before his public hanging Emmet made a defiant, patriotic speech at his trial to inspire later generations of freedom fighters.

In 1866 the Fenian suspects (► 56) were imprisoned here. In 1881 Charles Stewart Parnell (► 123) was kept here for six months, during which time he signed the No Rent Manifesto and negotiated the Kilmainham Treaty with British prime minister William Gladstone from his prison cell. In 1914 the gaol was converted into barracks to accommodate the extra troops recruited for World War I. It was reopened two years later to receive insurgents of the 1916 rebellion (see panel). After the Easter Rising, the War of Independence and the subsequent Civil War kept gaolers and executioners busy until the release of the final prisoner, Eámon de Valera (► 25). It marked the end of his second internment at

The 1916 Easter Rising

All those sentenced to death for their part in the Easter Rising were executed in the stone-breaking yard of Kilmainham Gaol (except Roger Casement, who was hanged in London). The list included Pádraic Pearse, Joseph Plunkett, Tom Clarke and James Connolly who, wounded and unable to stand up, was strapped to a chair before being shot at point-blank range. Plunkett came before the firing squad just two hours after he had married Grace Gifford in the prison chapel. Not only did these public executions make the 14 leaders martyrs, it did more than anything else to turn the tide of public opinion against British Rule. For this reason, Kilmainham Gaol holds a significant place in people's hearts today.

✚ 182 B2 ✉ Inchicore Road, Kilmainham, D8 ☎ 01 453 5984; www.heritageireland.ie 🕐 Apr–Sep daily 9:30–5; Oct–Mar Mon–Sat 9:30–4, Sun 10–5 🚌 Bus 51B, 78A, 79 (from Aston Quay); LUAS Rialto ♿ Moderate

Inset: Irish prisoners are released by British soldiers, 1920

The Fenian Society

The Fenians were members of an Irish nationalist secret militant group, formed in a Dublin timberyard on St Patrick's Day in 1858, and especially active in Ireland, America and Britain during the 1860s. From it the Irish Republican Brotherhood (and later the IRA) developed and, in 1905, one of its members, Arthur Griffith, went on to found the Irish nationalist party, Sinn Féin (We Ourselves).

Kilmainham: he had narrowly escaped execution in 1916 because he was an American citizen. Later he became both head of government and president of Ireland.

The gaol today

Following the closure of the prison, the building lay abandoned for decades and fell into decay. However, because of its exceptional historical interest, restoration work began in 1960 to preserve the largest remaining decommissioned prison in Europe. Entrance today is by guided tour only.

The grim, grey façade of the building sets the tone for your visit as you enter through the sinister thick door with a spy hatch that greeted the unfortunate prisoners at the start of their sentence. Above the door, five entwined serpents cast in bronze were known as the Five Devils of Kilmainham, and above that is the gibbet where public hangings took place. The main body of the prison – with its severe metal stairways, chicken-wired galleries and bleak rows of cells – contains numerous display cases with documents and personal mementoes of the inmates which retell the story of the struggle for Irish nationalism, along with various locks, shackles and the gallows. The guided tour leads you through the fearful dungeons, corridors and Spartan cells that still evoke a shudder and a sense of the building's tragic history as it portrays the tales of the people and force that shaped modern Ireland.

Robert Emmet

TAKING A BREAK

Enjoy a light lunch at **The Tea Rooms** on the premises of Kilmainham Gaol (tel: 01 473 2350, open 10:30–4:30).

KILMAINHAM GAOL: INSIDE INFO

Top tip Ask the guide to **shut you into one of the cells** to experience the grim reality of prison life here.

One to miss If you're pressed for time, skip the **audio-visual presentation**, which is the least gripping part of the tour.

② Guinness Storehouse

For centuries, *Guinness* has been synonymous with Ireland, and more particularly with Dublin. The stories of the city and Arthur Guinness's James's Gate Brewery are inextricably linked, and now one of Dublin's newest and most ambitious attractions has opened at the heart of the brewery. This ultra-modern museum provides a fascinating insight into the operations and history of *Guinness* and a shrine to the pint of what James Joyce so memorably called "the wine of the country".

The Guinness Storehouse by night – note the resemblance to a pint of the "black gold"

Early history

Guinness is one of Dublin's greatest success stories. In 1759 Arthur Guinness, a brewer's son aged 34, took over a small disused brewery here and leased it for 9,000 years at IR£45 a year. (The lease today is enshrined in the floor at the centre of the reception area of the museum.) After a short period of brewing ale he began to produce "porter" – a dark beer containing roasted barley – which rapidly achieved widespread popularity throughout Ireland and also captured a share of the market in Britain. Other Dublin brewers also began to make porter, so Arthur decided to brew a stronger beer called "extra stout

🚩 183 E2 ✉ St James's Gate, D8 ☎ 01 408 4800; www.guinness-storehouse.com 🕐 Daily 9:30–5 (9–9, Jul–Aug) 🚌 Bus 51B, 78A (from Aston Quay), 123 (from O'Connell Street); LUAS James's 💷 Expensive

porter", which involved burning the hops during production to provide a distinctively bitter taste. Thus he created the celebrated "black gold" of *Guinness* – a rich, black liquid, topped with a "foamous" (as James Joyce described it), creamy head. It soon became known simply as "stout", and its fame spread quickly. It is now consumed in many countries around the world. Arthur died in 1803, but he had 21 children and the brewery has remained in the hands of the Guinness family ever since.

There was no shortage of competition for the *Guinness* factory in the 19th century, with 55 breweries producing beer in Dublin alone, but there were plenty of consumers too. It is said that ale-houses formed one-third of the total number of houses in the city. Drinking ale was a regular part of everyday life. It was safer to drink than the contaminated water of Dublin, and even babies were given weak ale instead of milk. It is reckoned that at one point, more than a third of Dublin's population depended on the Guinness Brewery for its income – easy to believe, if you view the site from the north bank of the Liffey. From here, it looks like a great, sprawling metropolis, a city within a city. It even once had special trains linking it with nearby Heuston Station, barges that ferried barrels up the river and its own fleet of cross-channel steamers.

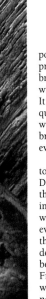

By the time the company was floated in 1886, Guinness had grown from its original site of 1.6ha (4 acres) to become the largest brewery in the world, with more than 2,600 employees. Today it is the biggest brewery in Europe, covering some 26ha (64 acres) of Dublin's city centre, with its own water and electricity supply. It produces more than 10 million pints of the creamy black stout every day, of which half are drunk in Ireland alone, and exports more beer than any other single brewery anywhere, to 120 countries.

Top attraction

Making the distinctive *Guinness* barrels

The state-of-the-art Guinness Storehouse opened in December 2000 and is one of the city's top attractions. A heady smell of roasting barley greets you as you approach the entrance and continue past a bulky, stolid skyline of chimneys, warehouses and vat-houses through the heart of the largest brewery in Europe. The museum building is a spectacle in itself, housed on seven floors of a magnificently converted warehouse. Instead of gutting and sterilising the remnants of industry, the architects have made them a feature with great steel girders left uncovered, and the defunct machines and vats left where they were or incorporated into the exhibition. The interior shell has been totally exposed, and rising through the middle of it is a series of rounded balconies that form the shape of a mighty pint glass.

The **museum** starts dramatically with display cases containing the various ingredients for *Guinness* located beneath a pounding waterfall. It is a deceptively simple recipe based on Irish-grown barley, hops, yeast and water which, contrary to popular belief, comes from the Grand Canal and not the River Liffey. The next few levels of the exhibition follow the course of a pint of *Guinness* through the brewery of the past, complete with sounds and smells: the clanking, gurgling, hissing and rumbling of the machines; the voices of the men who worked here; and the heavy, sleepy smell of hops, hot metal, sweat and steam. You can even walk inside the copper stills and the vats, capable of holding 405,000 litres – that's 720,000 pints of *Guinness*!

Other **smaller sections** are devoted to Arthur Guinness (► 24), cooperage, transportation, where models of ships, barges, carts and trains, and an original *Guinness* steam locomotive illustrate different modes of beer export, and advertising.

The Gravity Bar

Finally, lifts at the top of the building take you up to "the head on the building's internal pint", to the breathtaking surroundings of the seventh-floor Gravity Bar. They say that *Guinness* doesn't travel well; that it never tastes the same drunk outside Dublin or from a can. Where better place to enjoy a glass than at the brewery itself, and with astonishing views over the city?

TAKING A BREAK

The Guinness Storehouse has three bars: the **Source Bar** where you can relax with a pint of the "black stuff"; the **Brewery Bar**, offering contemporary Irish dishes; and the **Gravity Bar**, serving a complimentary pint of *Guinness* accompanied by striking city views.

GUINNESS STOREHOUSE: INSIDE INFO

Top tips The **admission fee** includes a complimentary pint of *Guinness*.
• There is an excellent *Guinness* **gift shop** on the ground floor.

Must see The **advertising section** consists of a huge display of ads over the decades, starting with the first, most celebrated one, produced in 1929, announcing "*Guinness* is Good for You".

Ones to miss The **Cooperage**.
• The **Learning Centre**: an entire floor devoted to teaching bartenders how to pull the perfect pint.

3 St Patrick's Cathedral

Not only is the handsome Cathedral of St Patrick Dublin's second great Protestant cathedral, the national church and the largest church in Ireland, more than any other building in Ireland it embodies the history and heritage of Irish people of all backgrounds from the earliest times to the present day.

Relics of the Knights of St Patrick

According to legend, the cathedral was built near a small well in which St Patrick is believed to have baptised his converts to Christianity in the 5th century. Today, a stone in St Patrick's Park, beside the cathedral, marks the site of the original well. It is said that the saint caused the well to spring from the earth and, for centuries, the water was thought to have miraculous healing properties. Because of this association with St Patrick, a small wooden church probably existed here as early as AD 450. The Normans built a stone church on the site in 1191, which was rebuilt in the early 13th century. However, by the 19th century the church had fallen into a poor state of repair and much of it was rebuilt in a major restoration project financed by the Guinness family. Sadly, little of the original building remains.

Cathedral treasures

St Patrick's most celebrated dean was the passionate social reformer, satirist and author of *Gulliver's Travels*, Jonathan Swift (➤ 23). He served here from 1713 to 1745 and is buried under a brass plaque set into the nave floor just to the right of the entrance desk. His self-penned epitaph, translated from the Latin, reads: "Here is laid the body of Jonathan Swift, Doctor of Divinity, Dean of this Cathedral Church, where fierce indignation can no longer rend the heart,/Go travellers and imitate, if you can, this earnest and dedicated Champion of Liberty." Buried alongside Swift is his companion "Stella" (Esther Johnson), with whom he had a long and apparently platonic relationship. His death mask, chair and writing table are also on display, together with his pulpit, a selection of his published writings and the parchment awarding him the Freedom of the City of Dublin.

Other noteworthy treasures include the 17th-century monument of the Boyle family; Ireland's largest organ; and a rare collection of memorials to Irish soldiers killed in British Empire

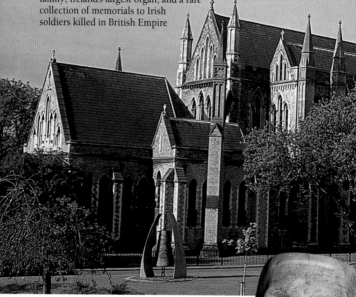

wars; and in the 13th-century Lady Chapel you can see the high-backed chair upon which William III sat when he attended a service here on 6 July, 1690, after the Battle of the Boyne.

TAKING A BREAK

Just up the hill from the cathedral, a tiny relaxing café called **Bite of Life** (55 Patrick Street, D8, tel: 01 454 2949, open Mon–Sat 8–4) serves delicious coffees, home-made soups, sandwiches, rolls and cakes.

✚ 184 B3 ✉ St Patrick's Close, D8 ☎ 01 453 9472; www.stpatrickscathedral.ie ◉ Mar–Oct Mon–Sat 9–6, Sun 9–11, 12:45–3, 4:15–6; Nov–Feb Mon–Fri 9–6, Sat 9–5, Sun 10–11, 12:45–3 🚌 Bus 50, 54A, 56A (Eden Quay) 💷 Moderate

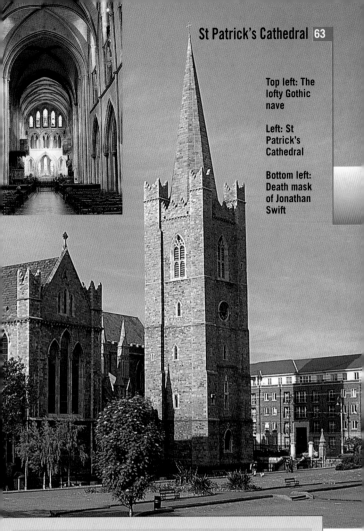

Top left: The lofty Gothic nave

Left: St Patrick's Cathedral

Bottom left: Death mask of Jonathan Swift

ST PATRICK'S CATHEDRAL: INSIDE INFO

Top tips Try to visit **early in the morning or late in the afternoon** when the cathedral is at its most peaceful. Alternatively, go at midday, as the tower houses one of the largest peals of bells in the country.
• Combine your visit with **Marsh's Library** (➤ 75) next door, Ireland's oldest public library.

Hidden gem The **memorial** to the celebrated blind harpist Turlough O'Carolan (1670–1738).

In more depth Living Stones, the cathedral's permanent exhibition, celebrates St Patrick's place in the life of the city, its history and its role as a place of worship in an ever-changing world.

4 Dublin Castle

Dublin Castle marks the centre of historic Dublin. For over 700 years it was the headquarters of English rule in Ireland, and Dubliners would joke about the figure of Justice over the main entrance – that she had turned her back on the city. Today, the hotch-potch of architectural styles, the faded brick façades and the tranquil atmosphere of the courtyards belie the turbulent history once enacted here.

The castle stands on a strategic ridge above the junction of the River Liffey and its tributary, the Poddle. It is thought that an early Gaelic ring fort stood on this site, and later a Viking fortress. The building of a medieval castle, with moat, draw-bridge and portcullis, was ordered in 1204 by England's King John, who required "a castle…for the custody of our trea-sure…for the use of justice in the city and if needs be, for the city's defence with good dykes and strong walls." The castle has been the seat and symbol of secular power in Ireland from that time until 1922 when it was handed over to the Irish Free State.

Throughout its lifetime as a British stronghold, various unsuccessful attempts were made to take the castle by such freedom fighters as Edward Bruce (died 1318), Silken Thomas Fitzgerald (1513–37) and Robert Emmet (1778–1803), and during the Great War of 1914–18 it was used as a military hos-pital. A further attempt was made to capture it by the Irish

Dublin Castle and adjoining buildings – a jumble of architectural styles

volunteers in the 1916 Rising. They gained
entry to the castle grounds and held out for
a day on the roof of City Hall before
being captured. Once the rebellion had
been suppressed, their leader, James
Connolly (► 25), was held in one of
the State Rooms before being
taken to Kilmainham to face
execution.

The castle today

Today's ensemble of buildings
no longer looks like a castle,
having been largely rebuilt in

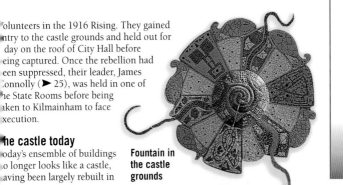

**Fountain in
the castle
grounds**

Dubh Linn

The city owes its name to the
"black pool" (*Dubh Linn* in
Irish) originally located on
the site of the present castle
garden. The pool was formed
by the River Poddle, which
still flows beneath the castle.
The Vikings once moored
their longboats here, and the
Normans diverted the flow of
the river to make their moat.

the 18th century as the political, judicial and
punitive centre for the Crown, with assembly
courts and offices clustered around two courtyards, together with luxurious ceremonial
apartments to accommodate the British
viceroys. Some of the rebuilding was
unplanned, as a fire spread to the Powder
Tower where the gunpowder was stored, blowing up a large part of the castle.

Little survives of the medieval castle that
once occupied the site of today's Upper Castle
Yard. The only visible remains are the base of
the **Bermingham Tower**, the curtain wall
beneath St Patrick's Hall, the foundations of
the Powder Tower to the north, and the lower
walls of the **Record Tower**, which today
houses the **Garda Museum**. Alongside the tower in the Lower Yard, the small,

neo-Gothic **Chapel Royal** was built in 1807 on the site of an earlier chapel with carved stone likenesses of British dignitaries outside and elaborate wood- and plasterwork within, some of which is painted to resemble stone.

Upper Castle Yard contains the castle's principal buildings. The **State Apartments** occupy the entire southern side of the yard and are used for such grand occasions as the inauguration of the president, as well as official entertainment, European summit meetings, peace talks and other State functions. They are sometimes even used as a hotel for heads of state and high-risk VIPs when they visit for discussions on the tangled issues of Ireland. A guided tour leads you through numerous palatial 18th-century rooms decorated with sumptuous period furnishings, vast Waterford chandeliers, hand-tufted Donegal carpets and grand Adam fireplaces.

At the end of the tour, the *pièce de résistance* is a visit to the **Undercroft** several metres below the yard level. Here you can see part of the original Viking fortress, the original city wall with its roughly hewn arches where the moat once flowed, and even a glimpse of the River Poddle, now underground.

Near the entrance to the State Apartments, the splendid octagonal clock tower (▶ opposite) is the site of one of castle's most puzzling crimes. It was from here that in 1907 the Irish Crown jewels were stolen while under a heavy guard. To this day they have never been found.

Below: Eighteenth-century life i. the courtyard

TAKING A BREAK

The **Queen of Tarts**, opposite the castle (Lord Edward Street, D2, tel: 01 670 7499, open Mon–Fri 7:30–6:30, Sat 9–6, Sun 10–6), is something of a

Seven Minutes Late

On 16 January, 1922 – the date the castle was finally surrendered to the Irish Provisional Government – Michael Collins (▶ 25), a prominent figure in the fight for independence, led the Irish army to the castle to take over from the British garrison. On his arrival, the commanding officer remarked "You are seven minutes late, Mr Collins," to which he retorted "We've been waiting over seven hundred years. You can have the extra seven minutes."

The Chester Beatty Library

The well-organised Chester Beatty Library – consisting of around 22,000 rare and precious manuscripts, books, miniature paintings and objects from Western, Middle Eastern and Far Eastern cultures – was bequeathed to the Irish nation in 1956 by Sir Alfred Chester Beatty and is considered among the most impressive collections of its kind in the world. It can be visited May–Sep Mon–Fri 10–5, Sat 11–5, Sun 1–5; Oct–Apr Tue–Sat 11–5, Sun 1–5. Free guided tours of the collection take place on Wed at 1 pm and Sun at 3pm and 4pm.

cult place for hot savoury tarts, wholesome sandwiches, salads and a huge selection of cakes and sweet tarts. Try the Baileys chocolate chip cheesecake.

✚ 184 B3 ⊠ Dame Street, D2
☎ 01 677 7129; www.dublincastle.ie
🕐 Mon–Fri 10–5, Sat–Sun 2–5; closed during State business 🚌 Bus 49, 56A, 77, 77A (from Eden Quay), 123 (from O'Connell Street)
💶 Moderate. Entrance by guided tour only

DUBLIN CASTLE: INSIDE INFO

In more depth The **tour of the State Apartments** includes the lavish Throne Room, the Ballroom (known as St Patrick's Hall), the Wedgwood Room, the Apollo Room, with its sumptuous stuccoed ceiling, the circular Gothic-style Supper Room, and the 30m-long (100-foot) Picture Gallery, which houses a collection of portraits of former viceroys, their coronets surmounting the gilt frames.

Hidden gem The ceiling fresco in **St Patrick's Hall**, depicting scenes from Irish history, is considered the most important painted ceiling in Ireland.

One to miss The **Garda Museum**.

5 Temple Bar

Upbeat, bohemian and youthful, Temple Bar is the city's cultural quarter – a lively district of contemporary arts and entertainment, with some of the best bars, pubs and clubs in town.

The compact, pedestrian-friendly district of Temple Bar owes its name to Sir William Temple, who purchased the land in the 16th century. By the mid-17th century it was Dublin's busiest marine trading area, with a bustling harbour at Wellington Quay. (The term "bar" means "riverside path".) But as the average

tonnage of ships increased over the decades, the low depth of the Liffey here forced the docks eastwards, and Temple Bar was abandoned for nearly 200 years.

A new look

It was the naming of Dublin as European City of Culture in 1991 that spurred the rejuvenation of Temple Bar, and the district has been at the epicentre of Dublin's revival ever since. The area has undergone a radical transformation: the former warehouses and merchant's houses clustered along the cobweb of narrow, cobbled streets have been rediscovered, renovated and redesigned with elements of bold contemporary architecture. Now it is the social heart of Dublin, and a gathering place for Dublin youth.

One of the main trademarks of Temple Bar is the large number of cafés, restaurants, pubs and bars (▶ 81–82), many of which host live music ranging from fiddle sessions to up-and-coming Dublin rock bands. The area is also renowned for its nightlife. In the early 1990s Temple Bar was in danger of sinking beneath a tide of wild stag parties and drunken weekenders drawn here from across Europe. However, the balance was restored with the introduction of a summer programme of free arts events, including street theatre and open-air markets. Now, there's always something exciting happening, whether it's street musicians, a music recital or an outdoor film-screening at Meeting House Square, or such special events as the Temple Bar Fleadh (pronounced "flah") in March or the Blues Festival in July. As the trendiest part of town, the district boasts a variety of unusual craft shops, boutiques and specialist markets (▶ 79–80).

Cultural centres

There is also a wide range of innovative cultural centres including the **Temple Bar Gallery** (5–9 Temple Bar), the **Graphic Studio Gallery** (off Cope Street), and the **Gallery of Photography** (Meeting House Square), all showing works by young artists and photographers; the **National Photographic Archive** (Meeting House Square), housing the photographic collection of the National Library of Ireland (▶ 105–106); the **Irish Film Institute** and **Irish Film Archive** (6 Eustace Street), showing independent and foreign films together with a programme of lectures and seminars, and **The Ark** (11a Eustace Street), Europe's first cultural centre for children, including an outdoor theatre.

TAKING A BREAK

You won't go thirsty or hungry here. Temple Bar possesses the greatest density of pubs and eateries in town (▶ 76–78 for a selection).

On the inside looking out – many Temple Bar pubs display fine stained glass

Temple Bar Information Centre
🞣 184 C4 ✉ 12 East Essex Street, D2 ☎ 01 671 5717; www.templebar.ie
🕐 Jun–Sep Mon–Fri 9–7, Sat 10–6, Sun 12–6; Oct–May Mon–Fri 9–5, Sat 10–6, Sun 12–4 🚍 All city-centre buses; Tara Street DART Station

TEMPLE BAR: INSIDE INFO

Top tip A free programme of events takes place during the day and evening. Full details are available from the Temple Bar Information Centre.

At Your Leisure

6 Irish Museum of Modern Art (IMMA)

The Irish Museum of Modern Art is Ireland's leading national institution of modern and contemporary art, where the work of major international figures is juxtaposed with the latest trends of up-and-coming local artists.

The collections are housed in the magnificent Royal Hospital in Kilmainham, considered by many the finest 17th-century building in Ireland. Designed by Sir William Robinson in 1684, and styled on Les Invalides in Paris, with a spacious quadrangle and elegant classical symmetry, it was a home for retired soldiers for almost 250 years until 1922. Later, it was used by the British as an army barracks. Only in 1986 did the Irish government restore the long-abandoned building at a cost of IR£12 million. It reopened its doors as the Irish Museum of Modern Art in 1991. Now its stark grey-and-white interior provides a striking backdrop for the permanent collection of Irish and international 20th-century art, as well as regular temporary exhibitions and an extensive community programme of music, theatre and visual arts. Look out for **The New York Portfolio**, an exciting collection of prints by prominent American artists, and **The City Drawings**, hundreds of drawings of cities around the world by leading Irish artist Kathy Prendergast.

Sean Scully's *Wall of Yellow Light* **(1999) at IMMA**

✚ 182 C3   ✉ Royal Kilmainham Hospital, Kilmainham, D8   ☎ 01 612 9900; www.modernart.ie   🕙 Tue–Sat 10–5:30, Sun and public hols noon–5:30. Guided tours: Wed, Fri and Sun 2:30; closed Mon, Good Fri, 24–26 Dec   🚌 Bus 26, 51, 51B, 78A, 79, 90, 123   🎟 Free

7 St Audoen's Churches

The Protestant **Church of St Audoen** is the only remaining medieval parish

church in Dublin. It stands on the site of a former Celtic chapel dedicated to St Columba, the patron saint of poets and one of the most revered of all Irish saints. Its 12th-century tower is believed to be the oldest in Ireland, and its three bells and nave date from the 15th century. In the porch, an early Christian gravestone known as the "Lucky Stone" – the subject of many strange stories – has been here since the 13th century. The church-yard is bounded by a restored section of old city walls. Behind the church, St Audoen's Arch is the only remaining gateway of the medieval city.

Next door to old St Audoen stands **St Audoen's Catholic Church**, dating from the mid-19th century. Its Great Bell is better known as *The Liberator*, after Daniel O'Connell (➤ 24). It rang to announce his release from prison and tolled on the day of his funeral.

➕ 184 B4 ✉ Corn Market, High Street, D2 ☎ 01 677 0088 ⏰ Jun–Sep daily 9:30–5:30, (last admission 45 mins before closing) 🚌 Bus 78a, 123 💷 Inexpensive

❽ Tailor's Hall

Dublin's only remaining guildhall, the Tailor's Hall, was built in 1706, making it the oldest guildhall in Ireland. In its heyday it was used by a variety of traders including hosiers, saddlers and tailors. One of the city's most fashionable venues for social events, it also hosted political gatherings – notably the illegal "Back Lane Parliament" meetings of the Society of United Irishmen, founded towards the end of the 18th century by Theobald Wolfe Tone (➤ 23), the middle-class Protestant attorney and father of Irish Republicanism. Since 1985, it has been the home of An Taisce – the Irish National Trust.

➕ 184 B3 ✉ Back Lane, off Christchurch Place, D2 ⏰ Closed to the public

❾ Dublinia

This state-of-the-art medieval heritage centre – named Dublinia after the first known recording of the city on a map in 1540 – covers Dublin's turbulent history from the arrival of the Anglo-Normans in 1170 to the reign of Henry VIII and the closure of the monasteries in 1540. Thrilling life-sized street scenes and audio-visual displays on the ground floor, combined with genuine artefacts from the National Museum of Ireland upstairs and a 1:300 scale model of the city, provide an exciting insight into medieval life. There's even a Medieval Fair where you can try your hand at juggling and brass-rubbing, or dressing up as a medieval knight. Kids just love it. The displays are located in the old Synod Hall beside Christ Church Cathedral, and the visit concludes with a climb to the top of St Michael's Tower for a dazzling bird's-eye view of the old medieval city.

➕ 184 B3 ✉ St Michael's Hill, D8 ☎ 01 679 4611; www.dublinia.ie ⏰ Apr–Sep daily 10–5; Oct–Mar Mon–Sat 11–4, Sun 10–4:30 🚌 Bus 50, 78A 💷 Moderate

Life in medieval Dublin is re-created at the fascinating Dublinia exhibition

🔟 Christ Church Cathedral

Christ Church Cathedral was the first stone building erected in Dublin. It replaced an earlier wooden church, built for Sitric Silkenbeard, Norse king of Dublin in 1038. The cathedral was commissioned in 1172 by the Anglo-Norman conqueror of Dublin, Richard FitzGilbert de Clare, Earl of Pembroke – better known as "Strongbow" – for Archbishop Laurence O'Toole (who later became St Laurence, patron saint of Dublin).

Over the centuries, the cathedral has been repeatedly restored and modified. In the mid-15th century, the cloisters were taken over by shops and the crypt became "tippling rooms for beer, wine and tobacco". Later, in the 19th century, the church was completely remodelled by architect George Street. Little remains of the original Norman structure, except parts of the south transept and the crypt. Unique in Ireland for its scale and size, the crypt is almost as large as the upper church and full of fascinating relics and statuary, including medieval wooden punishment stocks. Inside the church, look for Strongbow's memorial in the nave and the heart of St Laurence in a 13th-century metal casket in the chapel of St Laud. Nearby, mounted on the wall, a glass case contains the mummified bodies of a cat and rat, found in the 1860s. The rat was trapped in an organ pipe and the cat, in hot pursuit, got jammed just 15cm (6 inches) away from its prey.

✚ 184 B3
✉ Christchurch Place, D8 ☎ 01 677 8099; www.cccdub.ie
🕐 Mon–Fri 9:45–5, Sat–Sun 10–5
🚌 Bus 78 (from

St Laurence O'Toole's heart in Christ Church Cathedral

Aston Quay), 50 (from Eden Quay)
♿ Moderate

⓫ City Hall

Immediately after its construction in 1769, Dublin's City Hall was hailed as an architectural masterpiece and one of the city's most important public buildings. Originally designed by Thomas Cooley to house the Royal Exchange at a time when a revolutionary wind was sweeping through Georgian Dublin, the exterior marked the introduction of neo-classicism to Ireland and also set a new trend for copper-covered domes (see the Custom House, ► 133, and the Four Courts, ► 155).

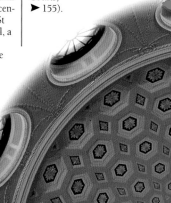

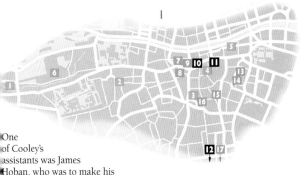

One of Cooley's assistants was James Hoban, who was to make his name a decade later by winning the competition to design the White House in Washington DC.

Today the City Hall contains the offices of the Dublin Corporation and a multimedia exhibition, "The Story of the Capital", which traces the evolution of Ireland's capital city from the early developments of the River Liffey to the present day. Here too are marble statues of Daniel O'Connell (► 24), Henry Grattan (► 89) and other important political figures, and the city's coat of arms and motto *Obedientia Civium Urbis Felicitas* (Happy the City Where Citizens Obey), depicted in mosaic on the floor of the dazzling, light-filled rotunda.

➕ 184 C4 ✉ Cork Hill, Dame Street, D2 ☎ 01 672 2204; www.dublincity.ie/cityhall
🕐 Mon–Sat 10–5:15, Sun 2–5
🚌 Bus 37, 39, 50, 50A, 54, 56A, 77, 77A, 77B, 123 💷 Moderate

🄓 Irish Jewish Museum and Heritage Centre

There has been a Jewish community in Ireland for centuries. Following the end of the Napoleonic Wars, there was considerable immigration from central Europe, but the main influx came between 1880 and 1910 when approximately 2,000 Jewish immigrants settled here from eastern Europe. They participated fully in all walks of life – in the professions, trades and manufacturing. Although only a handful arrived during the Nazi period, the Jewish population of Dublin peaked at approximately 5,500 in the late 1940s and this museum contains a fascinating collection of memorabilia relating to the Irish Jewish communities and their links to present-day Ireland over the past 150 years. The ground floor illustrates their commercial, cultural and social life here, including an impressive late 19th-century kitchen depicting a typical Irish Sabbath meal. Upstairs, the original synagogue, with all its ritual fittings, is on view together with the Harold Smerling gallery containing Jewish religious objects.

➕ 184 B1 ✉ 3–4 Walworth Road (off Victoria Street), D8 ☎ 01 490 1857
🕐 May–Sep Sun, Tue and Thu 11–3:30; Oct–Apr Sun 10:30–2:30 🚌 Bus 16, 16A, 19, 19A, 122 💷 Free

Flamboyant architecture – the City Hall's striking dome

🔞 Powerscourt Townhouse

This grand Georgian mansion was designed by Robert Mack (the architect of Grattan Bridge, ► 156) in 1774 as the city pad of Viscount Powerscourt, whose principal residence was in County Wicklow (► 146). It became a drapery warehouse in the 1830s, but today it has been converted into one of Dublin's most sophisticated shopping malls (► 79), cleverly combining the original façade, the grand mahogany staircase and some splendid stucco work with imaginative, modern interior design.

🔝 184 C3 ✉ William Street South, D2
☎ www.powerscourtcentre.com
🕙 Mon–Fri 10–6 (also 6–8 Thu), Sat 9–6, Sun noon–6

Viking roots to the 20th century, together with a nostalgic collection of old photographs, paintings, newspaper cuttings and maps. Don't miss the shoes of an ancient Irish giant, the model of the Howth tram and the sculpted head of Lord Nelson, which once stood atop Nelson's Pillar – a 40m (130-foot) Doric column in O'Connell Street, which predated the one in London's Trafalgar Square by several decades – until the IRA blew it up in 1966 on the 50th anniversary of the Easter Rising.

🔝 184 C3 ✉ 58 William Street South, D2 ☎ 01 679 4260 🕙 Tue–Sat 10–6, Sun 11–2; closed public hols 🚌 Bus 10, 11, 13 (O'Connell Street), 16, 16A, 19, 122 (George's Quay) 🎫 Free

Powerscourt Townhouse – a stylish shopping centre

🔞 Dublin Civic Museum

Don't let the dull-sounding name put you off, for a visit to this charming and intimate museum is one of the best ways to understand the psyche of Dublin and its people. Housed in the former City Assembly House, it is filled with a quirky assortment of objects recalling Dublin's past from its

🔞 Whitefriar Street Carmelite Church

St Valentine (► opposite), the 3rd-century patron saint of lovers, died in Rome, but his remains were returned to his native Ireland in 1836 and now lie in a shrine to the right of the high altar in this lofty church, built on the site of a former Carmelite priory. The church also contains an unusual oak statue of the Virgin (Our Lady of Dublin). The only survivor of its kind following the widespread sacking of Ireland's monasteries during the Reformation, it was found in one of the city's second-hand shops.

🏛 184 C3 🖂 56 Aungier Street, D2
☎ 01 475 8821 🕐 Mon, Wed–Fri 8–6:30, Sat 8–7, Sun 8–7:30, Tue 8–9:15, public hols 9:30–1 🚌 Bus 16, 16A, 19, 19A, 122 (O'Connell Street), 83 (College Street), 65B, 65C (Eden Quay) 💷 Free

🔟 Marsh's Library

Marsh's Library, Ireland's oldest public library, has hardly changed since it was founded in 1707 by Archbishop Narcissus Marsh, an avid collector of rare books and manuscripts. Designed by Sir William Robinson, the dark oak floor-to-ceiling bookcases contain a scholarly collection of 25,000 leather-bound publications, mostly from the 16th to the 18th centuries, including Swift's annotated copy of Clarendon's *History of the Great Rebellion*. Some of the books were so precious that readers were locked in with them, in the three caged alcoves at the end of the gallery. As an extra precaution,

the rarest books were chained to the walls to prevent anyone from "borrowing" them.

🏛 184 B3 🖂 St Patrick's Close, D8
☎ 01 454 3511; www.marshlibrary.ie
🕐 Mon, Wed–Fri 10–12:45, 2–5, Sat 10:30–1 🚌 Bus 50, 54A, 56A (Eden Quay) 💷 Inexpensive

🔟 Shaw's Birthplace

A simple wall plaque – "Author of many Plays" – marks the birthplace of George Bernard Shaw (1836–1950). His atmospheric childhood home near the Grand Canal Bridge at Portobello has been restored to its domestic Victorian elegance and, full of memorabilia relating to the life and work of the celebrated playwright, it provides a wonderful insight into the everyday life of the Shaw family. Here Shaw would drink "much tea out of brown delft left to 'draw' on the hob until it was pure tannin" at his mother's tea parties, as he began to gather the characters who would later populate his books, even though Dublin was never to figure in his writings. At the age of 20, Shaw moved to London, where he achieved tremendous success with such plays as *Arms and the Man*, *Man and Superman*, *Saint Joan* and *Pygmalion*. In 1925 he won the Nobel Prize for literature. Many of his works were banned within his home country during his lifetime on the grounds of blasphemy or obscenity.

🏛 184 C1 🖂 33 Synge Street, D8
☎ 01 475 0854 🕐 May–Sep Mon–Sat 10–1, 2–5, Sun 11–1, 2–5; closed Oct–Apr 🚌 Bus 16, 16A, 19, 19A, 122 💷 Moderate. Combined tickets available with Dublin Writers Museum (► 131)

Where to...
Eat and Drink

Prices

Expect to pay per person for a three-course meal, excluding drinks but including VAT

€ under €30 €€ €30–50 €€€ over €50

Not only does Southside West cover some of the most historic and fascinating areas of the city, it also encompasses many of the city's most popular cafés and restaurants, a fine selection of handsome and character-ful pubs, and the best fish 'n' chip shop in town. Temple Bar alone has more than 40 restaurants, chic cafés and bars within its narrow confines, ensuring something to suit every taste and pocket.

RESTAURANTS & CAFÉS

AYA €–€€

Ireland's first conveyor-belt sushi bar behind the Brown Thomas store (▶114) is just part of a sleek, cool café-restaurant serving traditional Japanese cuisine. Try the irresistible "sushi55" special offer on Sunday to Wednesday and Friday evening – all you can eat in 55 minutes at the conveyor bar plus one drink for €25. The adjoining deli has a good selection of takeaway dishes too.

✚ 184 C3 ✉ 48 Clarendon Street, D2 ☎ 01 677 1544 ◷ Mon–Fri 12:30–10, Sat 12:30–11, Sun 1–10

Il Baccaro €–€€

Located in a cosy 17th-century cellar, this bustling, informal taverna provides an authentic taste of Italy right in the heart of Temple Bar, and serves a range of hearty regional dishes from a weekly changing menu. For a light meal, try the generous platters of cold cuts and cheeses washed down with a carafe of cheap but decent house wine served straight from the barrel.

✚ 184 C4 ✉ Diceman's Corner, Meeting House Square, D2 ☎ 01 671 4597 ◷ Mon–Fri 5–11pm, Sat noon–11, Sun 5–10pm

Bad Ass Café €

This Temple Bar institution, housed in a converted warehouse, serves pizzas, pastas, burgers and salads in a buzzy, young environment and is popular with all age groups, but especially with children who delight in the entertaining menu, the colourful posters and huge cartoon pictures on the walls, and all the pizza spinning and tossing.

✚ 184 C4 ✉ 9 Crown Alley, Temple Bar, D2 ☎ 01 671 2596 ◷ Mon–Thu 11:30–11, Fri–Sat 11:30–11:30

Butler's Chocolate Café €

This small, modern, non-smoking café-cum-chocolate-shop is the ideal place to combine coffee-drinking with the taste and aroma of Butler's Irish handmade chocolates. Each cup of tea, coffee, mocha or hot chocolate ordered comes with a complimentary chocolate from the dazzling display counter.

✚ 184 C3 ✉ 24 Wicklow Street, D2 ☎ 01 671 0599 ◷ Mon–Fri 8–7/also Thu 7–9), Sat 9–7, Sun 11–7

Café Mao €€

You'll find innovative Asian dishes, a funky crowd and a great buzz at this simple, stylish restaurant. Don't be put off by the no reservations policy or the wait for a table, as once you're seated the service is swift and friendly, the menu exotic (Thai, Malaysian, Indonesian, Japanese and Chinese) and the dishes excellent value for money.

🚩 184 C3 ⊠ 2–3 Chatham Row, D2
🕾 01 670 4899 ⊘ Mon–Thu noon–11, Fri noon–midnight, Sat 10 am–midnight, Sun noon–10

Cooke's Café €€€

This fashionable café-bistro serves classic dishes with a modern twist and is frequented by such local celebrities as U2. The daily changing menu contains relatively simple food cooked extraordinarily well, with a varied choice of char-grilled meats, imaginative pasta and salad dishes made with market-fresh produce. The pavement terrace has a more informal menu.

🚩 184 C3 ⊠ 14 William Street South, D2 🕾 01 679 0536 ⊘ Daily 12:30–5, 6–10 (also Fri–Sat 10–10:30)

Eden €€€

This airy, two-storey restaurant with abundant greenery and an outdoor terrace makes an ideal place for an alfresco lunch, or for dining when classic movies are screened in the square on summer evenings. The weekly changing dishes make use of super-fresh, often organic produce and are artistically presented, echoing the restaurant's sophisticated, minimalist design.

🚩 184 C4 ⊠ Meeting House Square, Temple Bar, D2 🕾 01 670 5372 ⊘ 12:30–3, 6–10:30

Elephant and Castle €–€€

The Elephant and Castle is celebrated for its home-made burgers, giant bowls of salad and baskets of spicy chicken wings served all day. It's also hugely popular on Sundays for American-style family brunch. Book ahead for peak-time dining.

🚩 184 C4 ⊠ 18 Temple Bar, D2 🕾 01 679 3121 ⊘ Mon–Sat 8 am–11:30pm, Sun noon–11:30

Fitzer's Restaurant €–€€

A cool, stylish and uncluttered restaurant, Fitzer's is in a fabulous location overlooking the street entertainment and outdoor exhibitions of Temple Bar Square. This is one of three branches in the city (along with one in Dawson Street and another in the new Millennium wing of the National Gallery) serving modern, imaginative brasserie-style dishes, and with a brunch menu at weekends.

🚩 184 C4 ⊠ Temple Bar Square, D2 🕾 01 670 0400 ⊘ Daily noon–11:30

Les Frères Jacques €€€

Dublin's top French restaurant – noted for its classic, seasonal cuisine and seafood – is especially popular at lunchtimes with local business clientele. The exemplary service, candlelit tables and pristine white linen make it an ideal choice for that special, romantic occasion.

🚩 184 C4 ⊠ 74 Dame Street, D2 🕾 01 679 4555 ⊘ Mon–Fri 12:30–2:30, 7:15–10:30, Sat 7–10:30

Gallagher's Boxty House €

A hugely popular, traditional Irish restaurant specialising in "boxties" – griddled potato cakes wrapping up a variety of savoury fillings including beef and Beamish (stout), smoked fish, bacon and cabbage – and other Irish fare. The simple décor of pine dressers and bookcases creates a rustic, timeless atmosphere, and everything is served to an accompaniment of noisy chatter and traditional Irish music.

🚩 184 C4 ⊠ 20–21 Temple Bar, D2 🕾 01 677 2762 ⊘ Mon–Fri 9am–11pm, Sat–Sun 10am–11pm

Good World €–€€

When Dublin's rapidly expanding Chinese population want to celebrate with a good, authentic meal they come to Good World, where the Dim Sum is a real treat and duck and pork are house specialities. The place is always buzzing and busy and perfect for medium to large groups. If you're feeling brave ask for the "Chinese menu" and try something more exotic.

🚩 184 C3 ⊠ 18 South Great George's Street, D2 🕾 01 677 5373 ⊘ Daily 12:30–midnight

Leo Burdock's €

Leo Burdock's is the oldest and best fish 'n' chip shop in town. Be prepared to wait…the freshest of fish and huge portions of delicious crispy chips made from top-grade Irish potatoes are well worth it, and you never know who you might meet in the queue.

➕ 184 B3 ☒ 2 Werburgh Street, D8 ☎ 01 454 0306 ◉ Mon–Sat noon–midnight, Sun 4pm–midnight

The Mermaid Café €€

This popular bistro serves copious portions of home-made, American-inspired fare in a simple, uncluttered setting of wooden furniture with marine touches. Try the speciality Atlantic seafood casserole, followed by a platter of unusual Irish cheeses with spiced apples and celery biscuits. The wine list is as imaginative as the menu.

➕ 184 C4 ☒ 69–70 Dame Street, D2 ☎ 01 670 8236 ◉ Mon–Sat 12:30–2:30, 6–10, Sun noon–3:30 (for brunch), 6–9

Monty's of Kathmandu €–€€

The *Dublin Evening Herald* rates Monty's of Kathmandu as "the best ethnic restaurant in Dublin". Indeed, it is the city's only Nepalese restaurant and, with its extensive menu of unusual dishes, an absolute must for curry lovers.

➕ 184 C4 ☒ 28 Eustace Street, D2 ☎ 01 670 4911 ◉ Mon–Sat noon–2:30, 6–11:30, Sun 6–11pm

The Tea Room €€€

This ultra-stylish restaurant, with a menu offering the light, sophisticated dishes of modern Irish cuisine to match, is in U2's celebrated Clarence Hotel (➤ 40). The Tea Room is a great venue for star-spotting, and the wonderful gin martinis in the neighbouring Octagon Bar are reputedly Dublin's best.

➕ 184 C4 ☒ The Clarence, 6–8 Wellington Quay, D2 ☎ 01 407 0800 ◉ Mon–Fri 12:30–2:30, 6:30–10:30, Sat 6:30–10:30, Sun 12:30–2:30, 6:30–9:30

PUBS

For general pub opening times ➤ 44.

(See also **Pub Crawl**, ➤ 159–161).

Grogan's €

Small, scruffy, old-fashioned and located right in the middle of town, Grogan's (also known as the Castle Lounge) ranks as one of Dublin's best pubs. Its excellent *Guinness* and good *craic* draws an eclectic crowd of all ages and backgrounds, from old Dublin characters to the local art students whose works adorn the pub's walls.

➕ 184 C3 ☒ 15 William Street South, D2 ☎ 01 677 9320

Oliver St John Gogarty €

Poet, writer, politician, raconteur, sportsman and surgeon, Oliver St John Gogarty was all things to all men. But it was as a socialite and an avid imbiber that the city remembers him best. How apt therefore

that this lively pub at the heart of Temple Bar should be named after him. What's more, it offers above-average pub food on the ground floor – including such traditional dishes as Irish stew, Galway prawns, and beef and Guinness casserole – plus traditional Irish music daily on the first floor.

➕ 184 C4 ☒ 58–59 Fleet Street, D2 ☎ 01 671 1822

The Porterhouse €

Dublin pubs once brewed their own beer, but until the opening of the Porterhouse, it was a lost tradition. This creative micro-brewery serves around 100 beers including a variety of thrilling home-brews. Beer connoisseurs should order the special "tasting tray" of six different porters and ales, including Wrasslers 4X (said to be Michael Collins' favourite), oyster stout (brewed with fresh oysters), Wrassler and the extra-strong Brainblásta.

➕ 184 B4 ☒ 16 Parliament Street, D2 ☎ 01 679 8847

Where to...
Shop

This is a fantastic area for shopping between visiting the sights. Temple Bar is perhaps best known for its pubs and clubs, but this maze of streets, lanes and squares, popularly known as Dublin's "Left Bank", has plenty to tempt serious shoppers.

Treasure-hunters should check out the antiques quarter on and around Francis Street, while fashion fanatics should head to the bustling streets and narrow alleyways west of Grafton Street (▶ 105), which are becoming home to an increasing number of smart new designer shops. Here, too, you'll find the Powerscourt Townhouse (▶ 74),

a converted stately Georgian mansion, and the Design Centre.

FASHION & BEAUTY

Powerscourt Townhouse, the former mansion of Viscount Powerscourt (entrances in Clarendon Street and William Street South, D2, tel: 01 679 4144), is now a mini-mall containing up-to-the-minute fashions in its many boutiques, including **Occasions Couture** (tel: 01 707 9975), **Eden Park** (tel: 01 670 9012), **Jackpot** (tel: 01 679 4181) and **French Connection** (tel: 01 679 8199).

Several small specialist shops, such as **Courtville Antiques** (tel: 01 679 4042), **ESL Jewellery** (tel: 01 679 1603) and **Delphi Antiques** (tel: 01 679 0331), have handmade and antique jewellery on display, and at **Patrick Flood** (tel: 01 679 4256) you can watch the jeweller at work creating original pieces from platinum, silver and gold, which he frequently adorns with the delicate

patterns of his Irish heritage. But Powerscourt's *pièce de résistance* is, without doubt, the **Design Centre** on the second level (tel: 01 679 5718), containing the very latest creations of more than 20 leading Irish fashion designers including John Rocha, Paul Costelloe, Quin & Donnelly and Louise Kennedy.

Near Powerscourt Townhouse, **Costume** (10 Castle Market, D2, tel: 01 679 4188) is typical of a number of shops in the neighbourhood selling smart, highly individual separates and quirky labels, while **Susan Hunter's** tiny boutique (tel: 01 679 1271) in the nearby **Westbury Shopping Mall** is known for its wide range of sexy, self-indulgent lingerie.

In Temple Bar, join the city's trendsetters at funky clothing store **Urban Outfitters** (4 Cecilia Street, D2, tel: 01 670 6202), spread over four levels with an in-house DJ on the second floor.

For the ultimate accessory, head for **John Farrington** (32

Drury Street, D2, tel: 01 679 1899), and follow in the footsteps of U2's Adam Clayton, who allegedly spent IR£40,000 on an engagement ring for supermodel Naomi Campbell.

Feeling jaded after all that shopping? A visit to **Blue Eriu** beauty salon (7 William Street South, D2, tel: 01 672 5776) will pep you up with its cosmetics and skincare products from around the world.

VINTAGE CLOTHING

Dublin has always had a great choice of vintage and retro clothing stores. The best finds are at **George's Street Arcade** (South Great George's Street, D2), a covered arcade brimming with second-hand clothes and antique costume jewellery. Two great vintage clothes shops near the arcade are **Harlequin** (tel: 01 671 0202), which stocks everything from Irish tweed to leather and Chinese silk jackets, and **Jenny Vander** (tel: 01 677 0406),

Dublin's oldest antique clothing shop – a fascinating emporium filled with clothing and accessories from the 1940s and earlier. Charity shops scattered throughout the city are great places to spend a rainy afternoon seeking out a piece of classic clothing. **Oxfam** tends to have the best selection.

ANTIQUES, ARTS & CRAFTS

The Francis Street area has long been renowned for its antiques. One of the top stores is **O'Sullivan Antiques** (43–44 Francis Street, D8, tel: 01 454 1143). Other gems include **Odeon** (69–70 Francis Street, D8, tel: 01 473 2384), which specialises in art nouveau and art deco, and stained-glass specialists **Lord & Taylor** (106 Francis Street, D8, tel: 01 473 1883). During the summer, there is an **antiques fair** every second Sunday in Dublin Castle (contact Dublin Tourism, ▶ 37, for further details).

At the opposite end of the spec-

trum, **Designyard** in Temple Bar (3–4 Cow's Lane, D8, tel: 01 474 1011) flies the flag for new Irish design. This specially designed centre for innovative decorative arts contains silver, jewellery, furniture, textiles, glass and ceramics by Ireland's leading craftspeople. The ground-floor jewellery gallery sells the best of contemporary Irish jewellery in precious and non-precious materials, and the first floor features interiors.

Another specialist shop well worth a visit is **Daintree** (62b Pheasants Place, off Camden Street, D8, tel: 01 475 4641), which sells beautiful diaries, notebooks and cards by local artists. It also has the biggest range of handmade and unusual papers in Ireland, with samples from as far afield as Japan, France, Nepal and Mexico. **Crannog** (Crown Alley, Temple Bar, tel: 01 671 0805) specialises in contemporary Irish jewellery and ceramics. Their silver work is unique.

FOR CHILDREN

Pinocchio's (Westbury Mall, D2, tel: 01 677 7632) has Irish "collector" teddy bears and nostalgic tin toys, while the handmade wooden puzzles by Eamonn O'Callaghan at **Wood You Like** (Powerscourt Townhouse, William Street South, D2, tel: 01 679 4666) make unusual gifts for children, as do the jigsaw nursery rhymes.

FOOD

Dublin foodies spend their Wednesday and Saturday mornings at Meeting House Square in **Temple Bar** where the tiny artisan food stalls of the weekly market sell a wonderful selection of bread, cakes and pastries, fish, farmhouse cheeses, organic fruit and vegetables, olives, oils, chocolates, pâtés and terrines.

During the rest of the week, they head to **Magills** (14 Clarendon Street, D2, tel: 01 671

3830), Dublin's best-loved delicatessen, with such goodies as Hick's Irish sausages, herbs, spices, exotic sauces, salamis and their own home-made preserves.

Just round the corner, **La Maison des Gourmets** (Castle Market, D2, tel: 01 672 7258) offers delectable pastries and crusty French bread flown in daily from Paris, while **Vaughan Johnson's Wine Shop** in Temple Bar (11 East Essex Street, D2, tel: 01 671 5355) offers a huge array of wines from around the world, but especially from South Africa.

Further afield, the **Gallic Kitchen** (49 Francis Street, D2, tel: 01 454 4912), near St Patrick's and Christ Church cathedrals, is considered to be one of Dublin's best bakeries, with a small adjoining café that serves tempting home-made soup and potato cakes, coffee and pastries, and the most delicious *finnan haddie* (smoked haddock) quiche in town.

Where to...
Be Entertained

This area offers some of the most "happening" entertainment and nightlife. Nowhere embodies Dublin's celebrated carnival spirit better than Temple Bar. This small cobweb of narrow cobbled lanes, heaving with bars, pubs, live-music venues, arts centres and clubs, is where the city's heart beats loudest. In summer months (May to September) the area offers a free outdoor cultural programme with open-air street theatre, puppetry and street musicians by day, while in the evening, the best of contemporary dance,

theatre, music and film is featured in Meeting House Square and Temple Bar Square.

PUBS & BARS

Although Temple Bar was originally envisaged as a cultural centre, by night it is more like a social and entertainment park for the young set. By late evening, it's really rocking and most people are drunk. Hardly any of them are Irish though – the majority are tourists or weekenders on stag and hen outings from Britain. Party people and the young at heart will be spoilt for choice.

The following pubs are within a short distance of each other and all offer live music ranging from traditional fiddle sessions to jazz and

rock. The **Auld Dubliner** (24–25 Temple Bar, D2, tel: 01 677 0527), an old-style bar renowned for its local and foreign live bands; **Oliver St John Gogarty** (58–59 Fleet Street, D2, tel: 01 671 1822; ▶ 78), with hearty, Irish pub food and traditional music daily on the first floor; the **Temple Bar** (47–48 Temple Bar, D2, tel: 01 672 5287), with live Irish music nightly, good *craic*, a beer garden and a fine collection of whiskeys; the **Porterhouse** (Parliament Street, D2, tel: 01 679 8847; ▶ 78), a buzzy, multi-level pub with nightly live music and fantastic home-brewed beers; and the **Viperoom** (5 Aston Quay, D2, tel: 01 672 5566), a lively pub with a swinging late-night upstairs jazz bar. **Farrington's** (tel: 01 671 5135) and **Fitzsimons** (tel: 01 677 9315) in Essex Street East are also popular.

Beyond Temple Bar, **Bruxelles** (7 Harry Street, D2, tel: 01 677 5362) is a very fashionable, very loud watering-hole for students and tourists.

For something a little more relaxed, there's the more mature atmosphere of the **Octagon Bar** within the stylish Clarence Hotel (6–8 Wellington Quay, D2, tel: 01 407 0800; ▶ 40), owned by members of U2, thronged with beautiful people and famed for its unbeatable cocktails.

The coolest bar in the city for over a decade now, **The Globe** (11 South Great George's Street, D2, tel: 01 671–1220) combines a laid-back ambience with some of the best and most varied music in the city. Perfect for a coffee at noon and a pint at midnight.

Those who wish to sample the traditional Dublin pub should order a pint at the **Palace Bar** (21 Fleet Street, D2, tel: 01 677 9290), a former favourite of Brendan Behan, Flann O'Brien, Patrick Kavanagh and other literary giants, and one of several city pubs still with its original Victorian interior and mirrored panels subdividing the bar. You'll find some of the city's most sophisticated bars beyond the Temple Bar area, many of which have bar extensions till around 1:30–2am. Among the best is the **Capital Bar** (2 Aungier Street, D2, tel: 01 475 7166) – young, trendy, and popular with a superb upstairs cocktail bar – and **The South William** (52 South William Street, D2, tel: 01 677 5946) a cosy, upscale pub that also does exquisite gastro pies. The **George** (89 South Great George's Street, D2, tel: 01 478 2983) is a late-night gay bar with its latest craze on Sundays – "gay bingo".

4 Dame Lane (4 Dame Lane, D2, tel: 01 679 0291) is one of Dublin's best-kept secrets – chic, stylish and open till 2:30am, while minimalist, ultra-trendy **Dakota** (9 William Street South, D2, tel: 01 672 7696) is the ideal joint for chilling out. It's very popular with students.

NIGHTCLUBS

The greatest density of nightclubs is in the Temple Bar area, including

the **Turk's Head** (Parliament Street, Temple Bar, D2, tel: 01 679 2606), a lively basement club beneath the eponymous pub playing popular sounds and chart hits to a young, trendy crowd, while the hugely popular bi-level "**Rí-Rá**", meaning "uproar" in Irish (Dame Court, D2, tel: 01 677 4835), plays a hip variety of sounds – funk, house, garage, pop, soul – on different nights and is considered by many to be Dublin's premier club. Nearby, **SIN** (17–19 Sycamore Street, D2, tel: 01 633 4232),

Boomerang (Fleet Street, D2, tel: 01 677 3333) and **The Hub** (23–24 Eustace Street, D2, tel: 01 670 7655) are popular with the Temple Bar party crowd.

LIVE MUSIC VENUES

Dublin has had a thriving rock scene ever since local band Thin Lizzy made it big in the 1970s, and this area of town embraces some of the most popular live music venues.

Atmospheric **Whelan's** (25 Wexford Street, D2, tel: 01 478 0766) is a long-standing gig venue specialising in rock, jazz and traditional music, and featuring the best new Irish bands nightly and an after-hours club at the weekend.

Vicar Street (58–59 Thomas Street, D8, tel: 01 454 5533), the popular laid-back bar near the Guinness Storehouse (▶ 57–60), is slightly trendier, and provides a mix of comedy, traditional music and rock on Friday and Saturday nights, and stand-up comedy too.

For traditional Irish music, head to **Mother Redcap's Tavern** (40–48 Back Lane, D8, tel: 01 453 3960), a fun venue housed in a spacious old factory; the somewhat touristy **Brazen Head** pub (20 Bridge Street Lower, D8, tel: 01 677 9549; ▶ 153); or **O'Shea's Merchant** opposite (12 Bridge Street Lower, D8, tel: 01 679 3797), renowned for its very traditional music, its *céilí* (pronounced "kalee") dancing and its *craic*.

THEATRE & CINEMA

The main theatre in the area, the **Olympia Theatre** (72 Dame Street, D2, tel: 01 677 7744) has the feel of a Victorian music hall and specialises in comedy and popular drama as well as mainstream theatre, musicals, ballet and, at Christmas, pantomime. It also occasionally attracts celebrated Irish folk bands, and rock and pop artists. Most Fridays and Saturdays, shortly before midnight, the theatre is transformed into a lively late-night music venue with upbeat live music acts. In Temple Bar, the **Project Arts Centre** (39 Essex Street East, Temple Bar, D2, tel: 01 679 6622) specialises in more experimental theatre, while the **Irish Film Institute** (6 Eustace Street, Temple Bar, D2, tel: 01 679 5744), housed in an original 17th-century building in Temple Bar, shows mostly independent, art-house and foreign films. During summer months it screens classic films outdoors in Meeting House Square.

Southside East

Getting Your Bearings

Southside East is bursting with the colours, sights and scenes that encapsulate the very essence of the city centre. Just south of the Liffey, this has been Dublin's most elegant and fashionable area for centuries. Here you can marvel at the treasures contained within the cluster of museums, including the National Gallery and the National Museum; wander along the Grand Canal; enjoy the buzz of Grafton Street at the epicentre of the main shopping district; relax in quiet, secluded leafy parks; lap up the atmosphere at one of the neighbourhood's chic outdoor cafés or its traditional pubs; and experience the peacefulness of Trinity College right in the heart of the bustling city…and what's more, everything is within a few minutes' walk of each other.

This area also marks the epitome of Dublin's glorious Georgian era (1714–1830), best seen in the wide streets and the finely preserved squares and terraces that today form the main business sector of the capital. Of the several thousand Georgian houses in Dublin, no two doors are the same. Each has elaborately decorated fanlights, side windows, door knobs and knockers. The triumph of the Georgian terrace is each house's individuality, contained within a prescribed uniformity all based on the designs of classical antiquity. Indeed, it is these minute touches of personality – the ornate wrought-iron balconies, coal-hole covers and boot-scrapers – which are the rewards of a sharp-eyed visitor to this district.

LORD
EDWARD
ST

★ Don't Miss

At Your Leisure

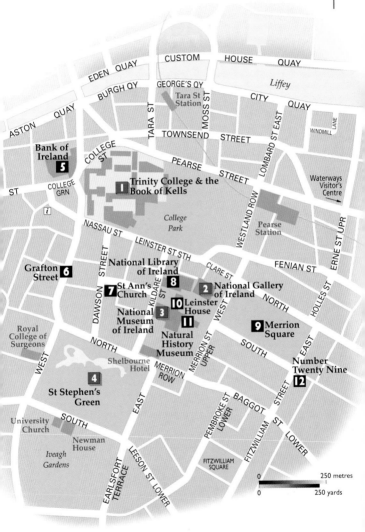

EDEN QUAY
CUSTOM HOUSE QUAY
BURGH QY
GEORGE'S QY
Liffey
Tara St Station
CITY QUAY
ASTON QUAY
TARA ST
MOSS ST
TOWNSEND STREET
WINDMILL LANE

Bank of Ireland 5
COLLEGE ST
COLLEGE GRN
ST
LOMBARD ST EAST
PEARSE STREET
Waterways Visitor's Centre

Trinity College & the Book of Kells 1

College Park
WESTLAND ROW
ERNE ST UPR

NASSAU ST
LEINSTER ST STH
Pearse Station

Grafton Street 6
STREET
FENIAN ST
CLARE ST
HOLLES ST

DAWSON STREET
National Library of Ireland 8
7 **St Ann's Church**
2 **National Gallery of Ireland**
KILDARE ST
10 **Leinster House**
3 **National Museum of Ireland**
11 **Natural History Museum**
MERRION ST UPPER
WEST
NORTH
9 **Merrion Square**
MERRION SQUARE
EAST

Royal College of Surgeons
NORTH
SOUTH
Number Twenty Nine 12
STREET
BAGGOT ST LOWER

WEST
Shelbourne Hotel
MERRION ROW

4 **St Stephen's Green**
EAST
PEMBROKE ST LOWER
FITZWILLIAM ST LOWER

University Church
SOUTH
Newman House
Iveagh Gardens
EARLSFORT TERRACE
LEESON ST LOWER
FITZWILLIAM SQUARE

| 0 | 250 metres |
| 0 | 250 yards |

11 Natural History
Museum ➤ 108

12 Number Twenty
Nine ➤ 108

Opposite: Grafton Street – the main shopping centre

Page 83: Southside East – Dublin's Georgian district

This makes a fun-packed day of sightseeing and shopping in the capital's most stylish district, climaxing in the evening with a "literary pub crawl".

Southside East In a Day

9:00 am

Start your day exploring the picturesque cobbled quadrangles and ancient playing fields of ❶ **Trinity College** (right; ➤ 88–93). The Dublin Experience (➤ 91), a 45-minute audio-visual exhibition tracing the history of Dublin from its origins to the present day, is a good first stop, before you view one of the city's greatest treasures – the magnificent 8th-century Celtic-Christian manuscript, the ❶ *Book of Kells* (➤ 91–92) – renowned as the most beautiful book in the world.

11:00 am

After coffee and a cake in Avoca Café (➤ 109), head to Grafton Street, the spine of Dublin's main shopping district, and watch the buyers go by. Then cut down Anne Street South and along Molesworth Street to the ❸ **National Museum of Ireland** (➤ 97–99) to view the dazzling gold and jewels of ancient Ireland. Alternatively, visit the ❷ **National Gallery of Ireland** (➤ 94–96), just around the corner on Merrion Square, with its excellent Irish art and an interesting European collection.

12:30 pm

Enjoy a relaxing lunch in one of the classy town-house restaurants on ❹ **St Stephen's Green** (left; ➤ 100–103). Try Thorntons, Brownes Brasserie or Shenahan's (➤ 109–112), or get a take-away from one of the sandwich bars and join the locals and the ducks in the park.

2:00 pm

You now have plenty of time to explore Georgian Dublin. **⑨Merrion Square** (left; ➤ 106), neighbouring Fitzwilliam Square and the streets in between form its heart, with their beguilingly elegant symmetry. Even though the vast majority of houses are now occupied as offices, it is not too hard to wind the clock back, especially on the quieter streets, and imagine you are back in a more refined era.

3:30 pm

Return to **⑥Grafton Street** (right; ➤ 105) to browse or shop in the luxury boutiques that flank Dublin's famous shop-till-you-drop thoroughfare. Then join other shoppers relaxing in the Lord Mayor's Lounge at **The Shelbourne Hotel** (➤ 111–112) – the perfect spot for a sedate afternoon tea with sandwiches, homemade pastries and scones with jam and cream.

7:00 pm

Go on the Literary Pub Crawl (➤ 168), starting in the Duke (9 Duke Street) just off Grafton Street. Actors on the tour perform scenes from works by James Joyce, Brendan Behan, George Bernard Shaw, Oscar Wilde and others, between leading you into various pubs for a pint or two.

9:30 pm

With the tour over, the night is yours. Why not continue pubbing? After all, you have over a thousand watering-holes to choose from in the city, so enjoy a night of mighty good *craic*!

⓪ Trinity College & the *Book of Kells*

Entering the peaceful grounds of Ireland's oldest and most famous university, with its glorious cluster of 18th-century buildings, lawns and cobbled quadrangles, is like stepping into a world far removed from the hustle and bustle of the city centre that surrounds it. Apart from a star-studded list of alumni, including most of the giants of Irish literature, Trinity College is best known today as the home of the priceless *Book of Kells*, the greatest Celtic illuminated gospel in existence, considered by many to be the most beautiful book in the world.

Trinity College

Queen Elizabeth I founded Trinity College in 1592 on the site of an Augustinian monastery – at that time the college grounds were outside the original walled city. It was during her reign that Ireland developed into a British colony, and her aim in creating Trinity College was "for the reformation of the barbarism of this rude people...to civilise Ireland through learning and to cure them of their Popery by establishing a true religion within the realm." Thus Trinity became a seat of Protestant learning. After 1873, Catholics were officially allowed to become students but, up until 1966, they had to obtain a special dispensation to attend on pain of excommunication. It is only in the past few decades that they

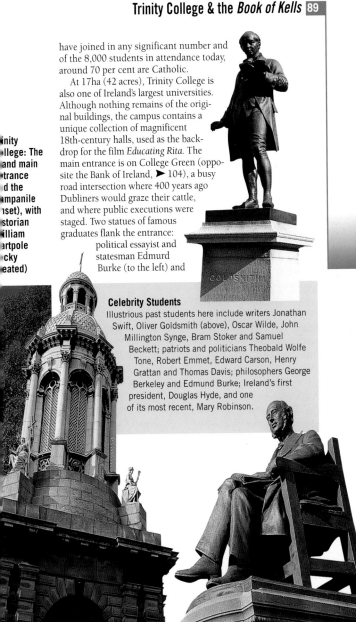

have joined in any significant number and of the 8,000 students in attendance today, around 70 per cent are Catholic.

At 17ha (42 acres), Trinity College is also one of Ireland's largest universities. Although nothing remains of the original buildings, the campus contains a unique collection of magnificent 18th-century halls, used as the backdrop for the film *Educating Rita*. The main entrance is on College Green (opposite the Bank of Ireland, ➤ 104), a busy road intersection where 400 years ago Dubliners would graze their cattle, and where public executions were staged. Two statues of famous graduates flank the entrance: political essayist and statesman Edmurd Burke (to the left) and

inity
llege: The
and main
trance
d the
mpanile
nset), with
storian
illiam
artpole
cky
eated)

Celebrity Students
Illustrious past students here include writers Jonathan Swift, Oliver Goldsmith (above), Oscar Wilde, John Millington Synge, Bram Stoker and Samuel Beckett; patriots and politicians Theobald Wolfe Tone, Robert Emmet, Edward Carson, Henry Grattan and Thomas Davis; philosophers George Berkeley and Edmund Burke; Ireland's first president, Douglas Hyde, and one of its most recent, Mary Robinson.

writer Oliver Goldsmith (to the right). The elegant, colonnaded façade hardly deserves Joyce's harsh description "a surly front, a dull stone set in the ring of the city's ignorance", but rather it sets the tone for the grand ensemble of buildings within.

On entering the college into the first quadrangle, **Parliament Square**, there is an immediate collegiate atmosphere – a sense of tranquillity and ancient seclusion. On the left, the chapel is the only church in the Republic shared by all the Christian denominations. The formal classicism of the chapel is almost mirrored on the opposite side of the square by the Examination Hall, with its noble portico, ornate ceilings and a magnificent gilded oak chandelier that originally hung in the old Irish Parliament. Both buildings, designed by William Chambers and dating from the late 18th century, are set off by atmospheric cobbles, antique lamps and cast-iron bollards.

Straight ahead of you is the most photographed feature of Trinity – a 30m (100-foot) **campanile**, donated in 1853 by Lord Beresford the Archbishop of Armagh, which tolls every summer summoning students to their examinations. Beyond the bell tower, the row of red-brick buildings (known as the Rubrics) with their unusual gabled architecture is the oldest surviving part of the college. Today it is a hall of residence. Pity the undergraduate living in No 25 – it is said to be haunted by an unpopular tutor who was shot by an anonymous student!

Beside the Rubrics, to the right, is the **Old Library**. Bear round the end of the building into Fellows' Square, a grassy quadrangle flanked by mostly modern buildings, including the **Douglas Hyde Art Gallery** and the venue for the **Dublin Experience**, a multimedia audio-visual exhibition telling the story of Dublin from its origins to the present day.

The entrance to the Old Library, the complex's earliest surviving building, is via the bookshop on your left. Here you will find Trinity's most precious treasure, the *Book of Kells*, and the splendid Long Room containing the historic university library.

Arnaldo Pomodoro's *Sphere within a Sphere* sculpture adorns one of Trinity's squares

The *Book of Kells*

Although surprisingly small, the *Book of Kells* is undoubtedly one of the finest manuscripts to survive from the first Christian millennium. It contains a lavishly decorated transcription, in Latin, of the four gospels, inscribed on vellum parchment and intricately ornamented with colourful patterns, human figures and exotic, fanciful animals. It was discovered in the town of Kells near **Newgrange** (➤ 149) in County Meath, but it was probably written by four Irish missionary monks on the island of Iona, off the west coast of Scotland, around AD 800. It is thought they fled to Kells in AD 806 after a Viking raid, and completed the book there. The Irish Church at this time was

The *Book of Kells*: Virgin & Child Enthroned (top); Christ with Four Angels (below)

largely monastic in organisation and the message of the life of Christ was spread primarily through gospel books, and the scribes and artists who produced them held an honoured place in Irish society. The book was sent to Dublin around 1653 for security reasons during the Cromwellian period.

Two of the book's four gospels are on view at any one time – one open at a decorative page, the other showing the beautifully rounded Celtic calligraphy with its richly embellished letters. Two other manuscripts are also selected for

Samuel Beckett (1906–89)

Nobel Prize-winner and contemporary Irish playwright Samuel Beckett was born in Foxrock, a southern suburb of Dublin. Like his fellow Irish writers George Bernard Shaw, Oscar Wilde and W B Yeats, he came from a Protestant, Anglo-Irish background. From 1923 to 1927 he studied Romance languages at Trinity College, where he received his bachelor's degree. He was also a keen member of the college cricket team. In the early 1930s he moved to Paris where he wrote many of his great works, including *Waiting for Godot, More Pricks Than Kicks, Krapp's Last Tape* and *Endgame*. Today the Samuel Beckett Theatre – part of the drama department on the Pearse Street side of the campus – stands in testimony to Trinity's great alumnus.

display from the books of *Durrow, Armagh, Dimma* and *Mulling*, each as old as the *Book of Kells*. They lie in a glass case at the end of an excellent exhibition entitled Turning Darkness into Light, which places the *Book of Kells* (and the other manuscripts) in its historical and cultural context. It also enables the visitor to view sections of the manuscript in much greater detail than would otherwise be possible, and to study the techniques used by the scribes, the colours (chalk for white, lead for red, lapis lazuli for blue, carbon for black and copper verdigris for green), the inspirations for their designs, the various symbols and the recurring imagery. The more you look at them, the more you see: sinners misbehaving, symbols of Christ (lions, snakes, fish and peacocks), angels, floral tendrils, and conundrums of geometry that resolve, as you stare at them, into elaborate initial letters.

The Long Room

Leading on from the *Book of Kells* display, the 18th-century Long Room with its hushed air and high barrel-vaulted oak ceiling of cathedral proportions contains more than 200,000 of Ireland's most important antiquarian books, manuscripts and historical documents, together with white marble busts of noteworthy scholars, including Jonathan Swift. This grandiose hall, 66m (220 feet) in length and 12m (40 feet) in height, contains a double-decker layer of dark wood floor-to-ceiling shelving in 20 arched bays, with leather-bound books, ladders and beautifully carved spiral staircases. With its stock of nearly 3 million volumes, it is widely regarded as one of the great research libraries of the world. Also in the Long Room is one of the handful of remaining copies of the 1916 Proclamation of the Irish, which signalled the start of the Easter Rising when it was read aloud by Pádraic Pearse outside the General Post Office on 24 April, 1916 (➤ 127). It's displayed to one side as you enter.

The splendid Long Room

TAKING A BREAK

Check out popular student joint **Nude** (➤ 111) or, for something more sophisticated, try **Dobbin's** (➤ 110).

➕ 185 D4
✉ College Green, D2 (other entrances on Nassau Street and Leinster Street South) ☎ 01 608 2320 🕐 The campus is open to visitors seven days a week 🚌 All cross-city buses; Tara Street DART Station

The Old Library and the *Book of Kells*
☎ www.tcd.ie/library 🕐 Jun–Sep Mon–Sat 9:30–5, Sun 9:30–4:30; Oct–May Mon–Sat 9:30–5, Sun noon–4:30 💷 Expensive

The Dublin Experience
🕐 Daily 10–5 (hourly shows), late May to early Oct 💷 Moderate

---

TRINITY COLLEGE: INSIDE INFO

Top tip Arrive early to avoid the crowds to see the famed *Book of Kells*, or visit out of season when there are fewer visitors.

Hidden gem Ireland's oldest surviving **harp**, upon which the harp emblem found on Irish coinage is based, can be seen in the Long Room.

In more depth Lively, informative **walking tours** of the college take place every 15 minutes during the summer months from Front Square. Ask at the porter's desk for information.

Must sees The *Book of Kells* and the **Long Room**.

② National Gallery of Ireland

The National Gallery houses Ireland's foremost collection of Old Master paintings. More than 500 paintings are on display with representative works from all the major schools of European painting, together with the remarkable national collection of Irish art from the late 17th century onwards.

John O'Leary

Thanks to a recent acquisition, three oil portraits of the Fenian patriot John O'Leary by John Butler Yeats are on show together in the National Gallery for the first time since they were painted. O'Leary became involved in revolutionary politics as a student and was arrested in 1865 for his inflammatory publications during the Fenian troubles (► 56). Sentenced to 20 years in exile, on his return, he established himself at the centre of Dublin's liberal nationalist circles until his death in 1907.

Masterpieces by: Vermeer (above left), John Mulvany (above right) and William Mulready (opposite)

The gallery was established by an Act of Parliament in 1854 and erected as a public testimonial to William Dargan, the designer of Ireland's railways and organiser of the Dublin Exhibition of 1853, a massive showcase of Irish craft and industry that took place in a temporary structure on the adjoining Leinster Lawn. Many of the paintings in that exhibition formed the nucleus of the early collection. The event inspired the assembly of works of art on a more permanent basis, to serve as an inspiration for up-and-coming Irish artists, and the gallery was eventually opened to the public in 1864, with just 125 paintings. A statue of Dargan, unveiled at the inauguration, stands outside the gallery.

The opening of an award-winning new wing in 2002 has greatly increased the size of the gallery and, since its foundation, the stature of the collection has grown considerably. Today it boasts some 2,500 paintings and approximately 10,000 other works in different media including watercolour, drawing, print and sculpture.

In addition to the national collection of European Old Masters, the gallery's main emphasis is on its exceptional array of Irish paintings (the majority of which are on permanent display), and the **Yeats Museum**, opened in March 1999 by the Taoiseach, Bertie Ahern. The museum is dedicated to the work of 20th-century Irish painter Jack Butler Yeats and his family – including his

brother, the famous poet William Butler Yeats. Look out for *The Liffey Swim* and various other Dublin cityscapes.

The European collections (Spanish, Flemish, Dutch, French and Italian schools) are on the second floor. Picasso's *Still Life with Mandolin* (Room 45); Vermeer's *Lady Writing a Letter, with her maid* (Room 40) and Velázquez's *Supper at Emmaus* (Room 33) count among the most celebrated European paintings, together with Caravaggio's *The Taking of Christ* (Room 42), a veritable masterpiece, found by chance in a Dublin Jesuit's house in 1990, which has since greatly enhanced the gallery's international reputation.

George Bernard Shaw

The playwright George Bernard Shaw bequeathed a third of his estate to the gallery, including the royalties from all his plays, as an acknowledgement of its role in his education. As a teenager, Shaw spent many afternoons visiting the gallery, claiming later in life that his time spent there provided him with a more enriching education than any he might have had at school or university. A fine bronze statue of Shaw can be seen in the Dargan Wing of the gallery.

TAKING A BREAK

Treat yourself to a light lunch of traditional Irish fare at the popular wine bar, **Ely** (➤ 110), just a stone's throw from the gallery in Ely Place, or enjoy a light bite in the gallery's café.

Every major European school of painting is represented at the National Gallery

➕ 185 E3
✉ Merrion Square West and Clare Street, D2 ☎ 01 661 5133; www.nationalgallery.ie
🕐 Mon–Sat 9:30–5:30 (Thu to 8:30), Sun noon–5:30. Guided tours Sat 3pm; Sun 2, 3 and 4
🚌 Bus 5, 7, 7A (from Burgh Quay), 10 (from O'Connell Street), 44, 48A (from Hawkins Street); Pearse DART Station 🎟 Free (small donation requested); Millennium Wing expensive

NATIONAL GALLERY OF IRELAND: INSIDE INFO

Top tips The best introduction to the paintings is to attend one of the **free lectures or guided tours**. Pick up a copy of the small magazine *Gallery News* for up-to-date details.
• The gallery also organises **family activity programmes** (Sat at 3pm) and, during school holidays, special "Little Masters" workshops and painting activities for children.
• **j3G** – the new interactive 3-D gallery with its easy-to-use touch-screen computer system – contains background information on a hundred of the gallery's finest paintings.

Hidden gems *Amorino*, a marble statue of Cupid by Italian sculptor **Antonio Canova**.
• **Room 15** (on level one) contains portraits of Irish people by artists from all schools.

Must see Don't miss the **Impressionist Collection**, with works by Monet, Degas, Pissarro, Sisley and others.

Ones to miss Most of the works in the **Print Gallery** and the **Baroque Gallery** are by lesser-known artists, although there are a couple of notable paintings by Rubens.

3 National Museum of Ireland

Not only does the National Museum in Kildare Street contain Ireland's most treasured antiquities, it brings to life the country's rich heritage and unique history from 7000 BC to the start of Irish Independence in 1921 through its magnificent collections, which include some outstanding examples of Celtic and medieval art and one of the world's largest and finest collections of prehistoric gold.

On arrival, notice the entrance hall – a dazzling domed rotunda with columns made of Irish marble and a mosaic floor depicting signs of the zodiac.

The first collection on the ground floor, **Prehistoric Ireland**, transports visitors back to the Stone Age, with its flints, vessels, tools, weapons and domestic objects, some dating from as early as 7000 BC. The huge Lurgan longboat – Ireland's earliest surviving boat (c2500 BC), hewn out of an oak trunk – is a particular highlight, together with a reconstructed neolithic passage tomb and a remarkably intact body of a man who lay for centuries beneath a Galway bog before being transported to the capital with fragments of his leather cloak.

Many important pieces in the museum were dug by chance from peat bogs that have natural preservative qualities enabling objects of metal, fabric and wood to survive in good condition for thousands of years.

Priceless treasures fill the museum's main gallery

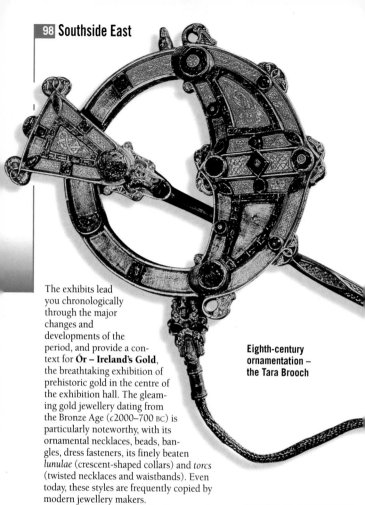

The exhibits lead you chronologically through the major changes and developments of the period, and provide a context for **Ór – Ireland's Gold**, the breathtaking exhibition of prehistoric gold in the centre of the exhibition hall. The gleaming gold jewellery dating from the Bronze Age (c2000–700 BC) is particularly noteworthy, with its ornamental necklaces, beads, bangles, dress fasteners, its finely beaten *lunulae* (crescent-shaped collars) and *torcs* (twisted necklaces and waistbands). Even today, these styles are frequently copied by modern jewellery makers.

Eighth-century ornamentation – the Tara Brooch

The greatest treasures of Celtic and Irish medieval art are displayed in the **Treasury**, to the right of the prehistoric collections, in particular the Ardagh Chalice, the Cross of Cong and the Tara Brooch. The 8th-century **Ardagh Chalice**, a heavily decorated, twin-handled silver cup, was found by a labourer named Quinn while digging up potatoes near Ardagh in County Limerick. Unaware of its true value, he sold his "treasure" to a local doctor for just a few pounds. The intricate processional **Cross of Cong**, with its beaded silver wire, decorative animal heads and inlaid enamel work, was made in 1123 for Turlough O'Conor, King of Connacht, to contain a relic of the True Cross. The 8th-century **Tara Brooch**, with its delicate copper designs set against a silver background, studded with amber and coloured glass, bird

Ten Years Collecting

A random selection of archaeological items found in unlikely places all over Ireland during the past ten years is displayed entertainingly in cabinets hidden behind closed doors. The intriguing labels – "in car boot sale", "in bag of potatoes", "upset by cattle", "amongst pub furniture" – entice you to open the doors and peek at the treasures inside.

nd animal ornamentation and
histle motifs,
epresents the
ummit of Irish
ewellery.

Upstairs, you can
xperience Dublin life
uring the **Viking Age**
AD 795–1170), with a vast
ange of fascinating items ranging
rom pots and pans, gaming boards, jewllery, toys, shoes, even Viking graffiti,
ug up in the Christ Church/
Vood Quay area of town.

The final collection (back
n the ground floor), **The
Road to Independence**, presents a vivid portrayal of Ireland's
olitical and military history from 1900 to the Anglo-Irish
reaty in 1921. The 1916 room is especially stirring, with "uniforms" of rebel Volunteers, the flag which flew over the
General Post Office (➤ 127) and a video wall documenting the events of the Easter Rising (➤ 54).

**The prized
Ardagh
Chalice**

TAKING A BREAK

The museum's café serves tasty
snacks, salads, sandwiches and
pastries. Alternatively, try
La Stampa (➤ 112) or
Jacob's Ladder (➤ 110)
close by.

⊞ 185 D3

◼ Kildare Street, D2 ☎ 01 677 7444; www.museum.ie ◷ Tue–Sat 10–5, Sun 2–5 ◻ Bus 7, 7A,
◻ (from Burgh Quay), 10, 11, 13 (from O'Connell Street); Pearse DART Station ▨ Free

---

NATIONAL MUSEUM OF IRELAND: INSIDE INFO

Top tips Many of the National Museum's collections, including all the decorative arts displays, have recently moved to the impressive **Collins Barracks**
(➤ 125). It is well worth the 2km (1 mile) trip across town to visit.

• A **Museum Link shuttle bus** (172) connects the three sites of the National
Museum at Kildare Street, Merrion Street (Natural History Museum, ➤ 108) and
Collins Barracks (National Museum of Decorative Art). Tickets and timetables are
available from the museum shops at Collins Barracks and Kildare Street (open
Mon–Sat 8–5:30, Sun 12:30–5:30).

• The museum offers 45-minute **guided tours** at intervals during opening hours,
lunchtime and evening **lectures** and a free **children's programme** on Sunday
3–4 pm (tel: 01 648 6453 for details).

One to miss Ancient Egypt (on the upper floor) has no Irish connections.

4 St Stephen's Green

This lush oasis of tranquillity right at the heart of the city, commonly called "the Green", provides welcome respite from the congestion of urban life and is a natural antidote to its noise, street and pollution. Beloved for its duck pond, its statues and its free lunchtime concerts in summer, on warm, sunny days, the park is filled with office workers, families and visitors sitting, strolling, picnicking and relaxing on the grass. No wonder James Joyce called it "the soul of the city".

The Green was originally a piece of common grazing ground and, close to a leper colony, it was used for public hangings. Building round the square began in 1663, when wealthy citizens could construct a house only if they planted six healthy sycamore trees on the Green. Before long, it became a private residents' square, and by the latter half of the 18th century it was *the* place for the aristocracy to promenade in their finery. The four sides, each nearly 500m (550 yards) in length, had their own named "walks", the most fashionable being the "Beaux Walk" on the north side, which to this day remains the most fashionable, overlooked by the exclusive Shelbourne Hotel (► 42).

St Stephen's Green was eventually converted into a public park in 1880 by Arthur Edward Guinness, the owner of the Guinness Brewery, who later became

ord Ardilaun. Today this 9ha
(22-acre) "National Historic
Park" holds a special place in
Dubliners' hearts, with its
manicured lawns, formal
Victorian flower displays, picturesque paved walks, ponds,
fountains and bandstand, not
to mention the memorials to
many of the city's famous
citizens.

Memorials

The park's main memorials
are located at the corner

In Memoriam

Look out for memorials to Lord Ardilaun (facing
the direction of the Guinness Brewery, the
source of his wealth), Countess Markievicz
(▶ 24), James Clarence Mangan (a local poet
who died in abject poverty), Fenian leader
Jeremiah O'Donovan Rossa, Robert Emmet
(▶ 54 and 56), standing opposite his birthplace at No 124, James Joyce (facing his former university at Newman House) and a Henry
Moore memorial to W B Yeats (▶ 13) among
others, all punctuating the landscaped lawns.

**Left: Lazy summer days
relaxing in the park
Below: Georgian architecture
encircles the Green**

entrances. The **Fusilier's Arch**, resembling a Roman triumphal arch at the
Grafton Street entrance, commemorates the Royal Dublin Fusiliers lost in the
Boer War. The **Three Fates Fountain** at the Leeson Street entrance was a gift
from the German people in thanks for Irish help to refugees after World War II,
while the modern memorial near Merrion Row to the "Father" of Irish republican nationalism, Theobald Wolf Tone, is better known as **"Tonehenge"**.

Notable buildings

Although St Stephen's Green is one of the landmarks of Georgian Dublin, there
was no overall plan to the buildings and the Green is notable for the variety in
age and style of its houses. The finest Georgian buildings include the Royal

College of Surgeons on the west side and Newman House to the south.

The internationally renowned **Royal College of Surgeons**, with more than a thousand students from all over the world, was designed by Edward Parke in 1806 and is one of the jewe[ls] in the city's Georgian crown, with its granite-faced, neo-classical façade and distinctive round-headed windows. The three statues atop the pediment are Hygieia (goddess of health), Asclepius (god of medicine) and Athena (goddess of wisdom). The building played an important part in the 1916 Easter Rising, when it was occupied by rebel troops under the feisty Countess Markievicz (➤ 24), and you can still see bullet scars on the façade.

The two restored Georgian town houses comprising **Newman House** (Nos 85–86) contain some of Ireland's most ornate 18th-century plasterwork. Look in particular in the Bishops' Room, Hopkins' Study and the Apollo Room, with its magnificent Apollo, his nine muses and countless cherubs. In 1865, the buildings became part of the first Roman Catholic university allowed in the city after the Restoration, although ironically No 86 was originally built

Below: The historic Shelbourne Hotel
Inset: Statue outside the hotel

for the vehement anti-Catholic politician Thomas "Burnchapel" Whaley. Cardinal Newman was the first re[c]tor, and the crouching lion on the façade has observed th[e] comings and goings of such notable students as writers James Joyce and Flann O'Brien; two leading figures in the 1916 uprising, Pádraic Pearse and Éamon de Valera; and the celebrated poet and priest Gerard Manley Hopkins, professor of classics here from 1884 to 1889.

Beside Newman House, the **University Church** look[s] nothing from the outside, but inside it is a gem of neo-Byzantine splendour, popular with students for marria[ge] ceremonies. Nearby **Iveagh House** was donated to the

State by Rupert Guinness, 2nd Earl of Iveagh, in 1939. Its interior, housing the Department of Foreign Affairs, is one of the most sumptuous in all Dublin but is sadly closed to the public. Hidden beyond Iveagh House is the lovely, secluded secret park of little-known **Iveagh Gardens** (➤ 20).

The most prominent building on the Green is **The Shelbourne Hotel** (➤ 42), a venerable Dublin institution immortalised in James Joyce's novel *Ulysses*, and the traditional place for old-fashioned afternoon tea after the day's shopping is done. For almost two centuries it has opened its doors to the famous, the influential and the notorious, hosting everyone from royalty to rock stars. History has unfolded within its walls: the British garrisoned the hotel during the 1916 Rising and the Free State Constitution was drafted here in 1922. But such was the service at the Shelbourne that, even when the Easter Rising broke out, tea wasn't cancelled. It was simply moved to the Writing Room!

Below: The Royal College of Surgeons

TAKING A BREAK

Take your pick from the numerous stylish restaurants fringing the square – **La Mere Zou** (➤ 111) is particularly good value for lunch – or have a picnic on the Green.

🚻 185 D2   ✉ St Stephen's Green, D2   🚌 Bus 10, 11 13 (from O'Connell Street), 14, 14A, 15A, 15B; LUAS St Stephen's Green

St Stephen's Green
🕐 Mon–Sat at 8 am, Sun and hols at 10 am. The gates are locked at dusk
🚌 Most cross-city buses

Newman House
☎ 01706 7422   🕐 Tue–Fri noon, 2, 3 and 4 (guided tours only)
💶 Moderate

ST STEPHEN'S GREEN: INSIDE INFO

Top tip At night you can best admire the **fanlit Georgian doorways** around the square, and also catch interior glimpses of the grand houses surrounding the Green, with their spacious high-ceilinged salons embellished with stucco-work, wood panelling and marble fireplaces.

Hidden gem The **garden for the blind** is laid out with scented plants that can withstand handling, and are all labelled in Braille.

At Your Leisure

5 Bank of Ireland (Parliament House)

The curving Palladian façade of the Bank of Ireland marks one of Dublin's most striking buildings. Originally designed by Edward Lovett Pearce in 1729 to house the Irish Parliament, it was the first purpose-built parliament in the world containing a two-chamber legislature. For more than half a century Irish affairs of State were governed from here, and within its walls in 1782 the Independence of the Irish Nation was declared. However, the building became redundant when, in 1800, the Irish Parliament was cajoled and bribed into voting through the Act of Union, shifting direct rule from

Above: Musicians in Grafton Street
Top: Bank of Ireland pediment

Dublin to London, thereby voting itself out of existence.

The Bank of Ireland purchased Parliament House in 1802 for

IR£40,000. During banking hours you can visit the House of Lords, with its original barrel-vaulted ceiling, oak and marble fireplace, glittering Waterford chandelier and massive tapestries depicting "The Glorious Defence of Londonderry" and "The Glorious Battle of the Boyne". The British Government insisted that all traces of the House of Commons were removed, but the mace, made in 1765, has been preserved in the "Story of Banking" exhibition in the adjoining **Bank of Ireland Arts Centre** (entrance in Foster Place).

🚩 185 D4 🖂 College Green, D2 ☎ 01 671 6801 ⏰ Arts Centre: Tue–Fri 10–4. House of Lords: during banking hours (Mon–Fri 10–4; also Thu 4–5) 🚌 All city-centre buses 🎟 Free

6 Grafton Street

Grafton Street is the capital's most famous shopping street, immortalised in many a song and story, and a "must see" for any visitor. Even if you don't have shopping in mind, it is so much part and parcel of Dublin life that just to walk it is an experience.

Pedestrianised and crowded from morning till night, there's always an electric atmosphere here, thanks largely to the talented street entertainers who draw crowds outside the high-street stores and exclusive boutiques that line the thoroughfare. But best of all, you can

never get weary shopping in Grafton Street because, within seconds of any store, there's always a tempting café or a snug Irish pub beckoning you in for a spot of refreshment.

🚩 185 D3 🖂 Grafton Street, D2 🚌 All city-centre buses

7 St Ann's Church

The best view of St Ann's Church is from Grafton Street, looking down Anne Street South at its striking neo-Romanesque façade. The church was created in 1707 for the rapidly evolving Georgian suburbs, with private pews to accommodate distinguished residents such as the Duke of Leinster, the archbishop and the lord mayor. The 18th-century nationalist leader, Theobald Wolfe Tone, married here in 1785, as did Bram Stoker, author of *Dracula*, in 1878. Dublin-born philanthropist Thomas Barnardo attended Sunday school here as a boy, before opening a boys' home in London's East End slums in 1869, which marked the start of a vast organisation for homeless children known as Barnardo's Homes. St Ann's also has a long tradition of charity work. In 1723 Baron Butler left a bequest specifically to provide 120 loaves of bread each week for the poor. Almost 300 years later the charity still exists, and to this day any person may take a loaf from the shelf beside the altar.

🚩 185 D3 🖂 Dawson Street, D2 ☎ 01 676 7727 ⏰ Mon–Fri 10–4 🚌 All city-centre buses 🎟 Free

8 National Library of Ireland

The National Library was opened in 1890 to house the collection of the Royal Dublin Society. From its foundation it has endeavoured to collect all material of Irish interest or of Irish origin published through the ages and throughout the world, and holds an estimated 5 million items on its 11km (7 miles) of shelves and in its vast archives.

It also administers the Genealogical Office, designing and granting coats of arms, and helping anyone with an Irish background to assemble facts about their ancestors.

You need to sign a visitor's book to get inside the main section of the National Library. Its real *pièce de résistance*, however, is the domed Reading Room with its narrow arched windows separated by pilasters that appear to lean inwards. It is especially atmospheric on a winter's evening with the green, glowing reading lamps and the impressive dome overhead like a giant, encouraging brain.

In 2002, the National Library acquired a remarkable collection of James Joyce manuscripts, consisting mainly of previously unknown drafts of *Ulysses*. Together with other material on the life and works

The Reading Room in the National Library

of Joyce, they are now on display in a semi-permanent exhibition at the library, providing a fascinating background to his ground-breaking novel (► 132).

🚹 185 D3 ✉ Kildare Street, D2
☎ 01 603 0200; www.nli.ie
🕔 Mon–Wed 10–9, Thu–Fri 10–5, Sat 10–1 🚌 Bus 7, 7A, 8 (from Burgh Quay), 10, 11, 13A (from O'Connell Street); Pearse DART Station
🆓 Free

🟡 Merrion Square

Merrion Square is one of the capital's largest and most impressive Georgian squares, with its typical four-storey-over-basement terraced houses with brightly coloured doorways, all in an excellent state of repair. Even though the buildings are roughly the same height, there is sufficient variance between them to please the eye. Notice how the windows on the upper storeys get progressively shorter. Not only was this cheaper on window tax, it also created an illusion of height.

The oldest, finest houses are on the north side, including **No 1** (guided

Off The Beaten Track

Anyone checking out the city's musical landmarks is sure to visit **Windmill Lane** (off Sir John Rogerson's Quay), where the band U2 made their first album at Windmill recording studios. Its walls are a spectacular sight, smothered in psychedelic, multilingual graffiti messages scribbled in tribute to the city's musical heroes.

Nearby, the **Waterways Visitor Centre** on the Grand Canal houses an interactive multimedia exhibition exploring Ireland's inland waterways, their historical background and their modern amenity uses (tel: 01 677 7510, open daily 9:30–5:30, Jun–Sep; Wed–Sun 12:30–5, rest of year, Grand Canal DART Station). From here, it is a pleasant two-hour stroll along the Grand Canal's towpath to Kilmainham.

The **Tower Design Centre**, in a converted 19th-century sugar-refining tower opposite the Waterway's Visitor Centre, contains more than 30 separate craft enterprises producing fine souvenirs in stained glass, knitwear, painted silk, pottery and jewellery.

tours Mon, Wed and Thu 10–noon, inexpensive), the childhood home of Oscar Wilde, one of the world's greatest wits and most popular playwrights. Over the years, the square has been home to several prominent Dubliners: **No 58** was the home of Daniel O'Connell; the writer Joseph Sheridan Le Fanu lived at **No 70**; and W B Yeats at **No 82**. In the northeastern corner, the **National Maternity Hospital**, founded initially in 1884, is eye-catching for its neo-Georgian façade. To the west, the square is dominated by the National Gallery of Ireland (► 94–96) and Leinster House (► right).

The delightful flower-filled green is one of the most attractive parks in town, far removed from its role in the 1840s as an emergency soup kitchen during the Great Famine. Today, you'll find busts of Michael Collins and Henry Grattan amid the trees, as well as a flamboyant statue of Wilde opposite his home. The paths are lined with an odd assortment of street lamps: the city has always had a variety of street lighting and one example of each type has been placed here.

Oscar Wilde spent his formative years in Merrion Square

🚇 185 E3   ✉ Merrion Square, D2
🚌 Bus 5, 7, 7A (from Burgh Quay), 10 (from O'Connell Street), 44, 48A (from Hawkins Street); Pearse DART Station

🔟 Leinster House

Leinster House is arguably Dublin's finest Georgian town house. When, in 1745, the Earl of Kildare built Kildare House on a greenfield

site just south of Trinity College, many others followed his example, hence the numerous Georgian avenues and squares of the neighbourhood. The house was renamed after the Earl became Duke of Leinster in 1766. It was the largest Georgian town house in Ireland. The Duke reputedly never liked it, nor could he agree with his architect, Richard Castle, which side should be the front, so both sides were decided upon: the Kildare Street façade has the appearance of a large, ornate town house, while the Merrion Square façade resembles more a country estate. In 1922, the house was acquired by the Irish Free State, and today houses *An Dáil Éireann* – the Irish Parliament.

🔢 185 D3 ✉ Kildare Street, D2
☎ 01 619 4057 ⏰ Guided tours Sat
10:30 and 2:15 🚌 Bus 7, 7A, 8 (from
Burgh Quay), 10, 11, 13A (from O'Connell
Street); Pearse DART Station

🔟 Natural History Museum

This marvellous zoological museum was inaugurated in 1857, when Dr David Livingstone delivered the opening lecture on his "African discoveries". It is among the world's finest and most comprehensive collections of stuffed animals, which are displayed in old Victorian cabinets. With more than 2 million species (of which roughly half are insects), it still has the

ability to inspire wonder and amazement in young and old alike, despite its nickname – "the dead zoo". The ground-floor Irish Room illustrates the country's astonishing variety of wildlife, while the World Animals Collection on the upper floor and galleries contains specimens from every corner of the globe, including a skeleton of a 22m (72-foot) fin whale, beached in County Sligo, and now suspended from the roof.

🔢 185 E3 ✉ Merrion Street, D2
☎ 01 677 7444 ⏰ Tue–Sat 10–5, Sun
2–5 🚌 Bus 7, 7A, 8 (from Burgh Quay)
🎟 Free

🔢 Number Twenty Nine

This magnificent corner town house has been perfectly restored and sumptuously decorated in the style of the period 1790 to 1820, to provide visitors with a rare insight into the life of a typical middle-class family in the late Georgian era.

The first owner of Number Twenty Nine was a widow, Mrs Olivia Beatty, who bought the house in 1794 for £320 and moved in with her three children. An audio-visual show at the start of the tour introduces you to her and her late husband, a wine merchant and paper manufacturer. The tour then leads from the basement servants' quarters to the attic playroom, through the narrow five-storey house with its original fittings and period furniture, which so vividly recapture the atmosphere of Olivia's home. Look out for the petticoat mirror, the rat shelf in the pantry, the primitive water filter and whale-oil lamps, the pet cricket cage (to bring good luck), the ruff irons, Waterford glass hot-toddy measures, and even a primitive fitness machine – it is these everyday items that really bring the house to life.

🔢 185 E2 ✉ 29 Fitzwilliam
Street Lower, D2 ☎ 01 702 6165
⏰ Tue–Sat 10–5, Sun 2–5 🚌 Bus 6,
7, 8, 10, 45; Pearse DART Station
🎟 Inexpensive

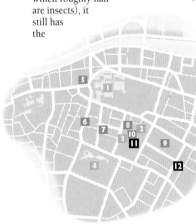

Where to...
Eat and Drink

Prices
Expect to pay per person for a three-course meal, excluding drinks but including VAT
€ under €30   €€ €30–50   €€€ over €50

Southside East contains some of the best options for eating and drinking. For gourmets, there are two of Dublin's most expensive restaurants – Patrick Guilbaud and Thornton's – and a host of classy town-house restaurants in the Georgian districts and around St Stephen's Green. The area also boasts a variety of good mid-price options, not to mention several chic cafés, popular wine-bars, buzzy coffee shops and some of the city's most outstanding traditional pubs.

RESTAURANTS & CAFÉS

Avoca Café €
Avoca Handweavers, the renowned craftshop that has its flagship store in County Wicklow, has opened a large store in the city centre (▶ 114) with a café on the top floor. Among the fare served are warming, hearty home-made soups, creative fresh salads, freshly squeezed fruit juices, coffee, tea and deliciously tempting cream cakes.
185 D4 ☒ 11–13 Suffolk Street, D2 ☎ 01 672 6019 ◉ Mon–Wed and Sat 10–6, Thu 10–8, Sun 11–6

Brownes Brasserie €€€
Sophisticated dining in a grand Georgian town house overlooking the Green between The Shelbourne Hotel and Grafton Street, with plush velvet banquettes, starched white linen, mirrors, friezes and chandeliers. The cooking is eclectic and refined, leaning heavily on aromatic Mediterranean dishes with bold, sun-drenched colours and strong earthy flavours. The wine list is equally impressive.
185 D3 ☒ 22 St Stephen's Green, D2 ☎ 01 638 3939 ◉ Sun–Fri 12:30–3, 6:30–11 (10 on Sun)

La Cave €€
Full of atmosphere, the capital's oldest French-style wine bar serves simple bistro fare at affordable prices with a wine list of more than 275 wines. Everything is squeezed into a tiny basement and nostalgically decorated with bistro clichés – *fin-de-siècle* posters, wine labels, red-and-white checked table-cloths and candles. It is especially popular for post-theatre, late-night dining.
185 D3 ☒ 28 Anne Street South, D2 ☎ 01 679 4409 ◉ Mon–Sat 12:30pm–2:30am, Sun 6–2:30

The Chili Club €€
This small, intimate restaurant hidden in a side street off Grafton Street was Dublin's first authentic Thai restaurant. The service is friendly and attentive, while the cuisine is genuine Thai.
185 D3 ☒ 1 Anne's Lane, Anne Street South, D2 ☎ 01 677 3721 ◉ Mon–Sat 12:30–2:30, 6–11, Sun 6–11

Diep Le Shaker €€
Forget the mini pagodas and Chinese dragons on the walls

the floor. Gary Flynn, head chef since 1985, has attracted a loyal following of businesspeople, politicians and locals thanks to his consistently fine international cuisine and one of the best wine lists in town.

🚩 185 F2 ⊠ 15 Stephen's Lane, D2 ☎ 01 676 4670 ◉ Tue–Fri 12:30–2:30, 7–10, Sat 7–10, Mon 12:30–2:30

Dunne and Cressenzi €-€€

The unpretentious brilliance of this brother and sister Italian restaurant and deli has made it one of the most popular eateries in the city centre. The simple menu (paninis, antipasti, a single pasta special and desserts) belies the quality of everything on your plate. The top-notch wine list helps to give the place a nice little buzz as groups linger at the long tables. The atmosphere is casual but classy.

🚩 185 D3 ⊠ 14 South Fredrick Street, D2 ☎ 01 661 1829 ◉ Daily 12:30–10

---

because Diep's is a Chinese restaurant with a difference. This light, bright, two-storey restaurant near Fitzwilliam Square, with its voguish cocktail bar, its butter-yellow walls, modern red-and-yellow velvet chairs and starched white linen, evokes a mood of comfortable glamour and relaxed sophistication. The menu offers equally stylish Asian cuisine: Chinese dishes are marked in blue on the menu, Thai dishes in red.

🚩 185 E2 ⊠ 55 Pembroke Lane (off Pembroke Street), D2 ☎ 01 661 1829 ◉ Mon–Thu 6:30–10:30, Fri–Sat 6:30–11:15

Dobbin's Wine Bistro €€

They say this hallowed establishment invented the concept of "doing lunch" in Dublin, and it is easy to believe when you step inside this sociable yet intimate bistro with its arched brick ceiling, its jolly red-and-white-gingham tablecloths and sawdust strewn on

L'Ecrivain €-€€€

Derry Clarke is undoubtedly one of Dublin's most acclaimed chefs. His cooking style is "New Irish Cuisine" with Mediterranean influences, and he always uses the freshest of local produce to create exquisite flavour combinations, as exemplified in his signature dish – baked rock oysters with cured bacon, cabbage and a Guinness sabayon. A further litany of delights includes a wonderful warm chocolate fondant with pistachio and zabaglione ice creams. The restaurant is light, airy and sophisticated, with plenty of pale wood, cream fabrics and formal table settings, and the wine list is tremendous. Portraits of Irish writers adorn the walls and a bronze of Brendan Behan greets you in the reception area. The balcony is especially popular for alfresco dining in summer.

🚩 185 E2 ⊠ 109a Baggot Street Lower, D2 ☎ 01 661 1919 ◉ Mon–Fri 12:30–2, Mon–Sat 7–11

Ely €-€€

This popular, contemporary wine bar occupies the ground floor and basement of a stylishly renovated Georgian town house, and serves up excellent Irish fare from the owner's organic farm at lunchtime and dinner – soups, sausage and mash, Irish stew made with organic lamb, local oysters and genuine Dublin coddle (bacon, bangers and spuds) – with 60 different wines served by the glass. There's live jazz on Saturdays at 10:30pm and also on Sundays to accompany the sensational brunch.

🚩 185 D2 ⊠ 22 Ely Place, D2 ☎ 01 676 8986 ◉ Mon–Thu noon–11:30, Fri–Sat noon–12:30 am

Jacob's Ladder €€-€€€

This stylish, minimalist first-floor restaurant overlooks the playing fields of Trinity College. It serves imaginative, seasonal New Irish cuisine, with a great "early bird" menu (Mon–Fri 6–7pm). The shellfish coddle – a modern version of the traditional Dublin dish – is recommended.

✚ 185 D3 ✉ 4 Nassau Street, D2
☎ 01 670 3865 ⊙ Tue–Fri 12:30–2:30, 6–10, Sat 12:30–2:30, 7–10

Kilkenny €

The wholesome quiches, stews, soups, sandwiches, home-baked breads and cakes of this busy self-service restaurant on the first floor of the celebrated Irish design shop (▲ 114) make an ideal shoppers' lunch. The ingredients are all fresh and additive-free and the store sells a range of Kilkenny preserves and dressings in the shop below.

✚ 185 D3 ✉ 6 Nassau Street, D2
☎ 01 677 7066 ⊙ Mon–Fri 8:30–6 (also Thu 6–8), Sat 9–6, Sun 11–6

La Mere Zou €€

A small, well-regarded restaurant serving classical French cuisine in a Georgian basement on the north side of the Green. The ambience is rustic and relaxed – distinctly

Provençale in its choice of sunny red, yellow and pale blue décor – with lavish bowls of fruit and freshly cut flowers, and cafe-style newspapers on sticks. Service is friendly and efficient, the food is good value (especially the lunch menus) and the wine list contains an excellent selection of French regional wines.

✚ 185 D3 ✉ 22 St Stephen's Green, D2 ☎ 01 661 6669 ⊙ Mon–Fri 12:30–2:30, Mon–Sat 6–10:30, Sun 6–9:30

Nude €

The home-made soups, hot and cold wraps, organic snacks, juices and smoothies at this hip snack bar near Trinity College and Grafton Street provide a pleasant alternative to sandwiches for lunch.

✚ 185 D4 ✉ 21 Suffolk Street, D2 ☎ 01 677 4804 ⊙ Mon–Fri 7:30am–9pm, Sat 11–9

Pasta Fresca €

A long-established restaurant-cum-delicatessen situated just off

Grafton Street. The shop sells fresh home-made pasta, sauces, oils and its own Caffe Fresca coffee, while the restaurant specialises in Italian cuisine, including a good choice of vegetarian options and delicious salad combinations. Open all day, and constantly busy, its lunch deals are especially popular with locals and visitors alike.

✚ 184 C3 ✉ 3–4 Chatham Street, D2 ☎ 01 679 2402 ⊙ Mon–Thu 11am–11:30pm, Fri–Sat 11am–midnight, Sun 1–10

Patrick Guilbaud €€€

One of the top restaurants in town (it's located in the Merrion hotel; ▲ 41), with prices to match, Patrick Guilbaud is celebrated for its dazzling fusion of contemporary French haute cuisine with Irish influences using Irish produce in season. Dining here is ultra-formal, the service meticulous and the food refreshingly simple. The lunch menu is especially popular with business clients.

✚ 185 E3 ✉ Merrion Hotel, 21 Merrion Street Upper, D2 ☎ 01 676 4192 ⊙ Tue–Sat 12:30–2, 7:30–10:15

Roly's Bistro €€

Large, loud and lively, this two-storey bistro in Ballsbridge, serving French, Irish and international classics, is rated among the top eateries in town. Specialities include Clonakilty black pudding wrapped in brioche, Kerry lamb pie, and Dublin Bay prawns with garlic, chilli and lemon. Booking is essential.

✚ 186 B1 ✉ 7 Ballsbridge Terrace, D4 ☎ 01 668 2611 ⊙ Daily noon–3, 6–10

The Shelbourne Hotel €–€€

No visit to Dublin would be complete without traditional after-noon tea at this historic hotel (▲ 42) – fancy sandwiches, scones and cakes in the plush surroundings of the celebrated Lord Mayor's Lounge, where the

Irish Constitution was written in 1922. For pre-dinner drinks, try the dark, glitzy **Horseshoe Bar**, a long-time favourite watering-hole for politicians, media and showbiz folk, before dining at the hotel's main restaurant, No 27 The Green.

➕ 185 D3 ⊠ 27 St Stephen's Green, D2 ☎ 01 663 4500 ⏰ Tea 3–5

Shenahan's €€€

This American-style steakhouse, set in a gracious Georgian mansion, is known for its Certified Irish Angus Beef, its exceptionally fresh Atlantic seafood and an impressive wine list. Before your meal, enjoy an aperitif in the Oval Office – a bar decorated with memorabilia commemorating some of the American presidents with Irish connections.

➕ 185 D3 ⊠ 119 St Stephen's Green, D2 ☎ 01 407 0939 ⏰ Sat–Thu 6–10, Fri 12:30–2, 6–10

La Stampa €€€–€€€

This sumptuous *belle époque* dining-room with its high curved ceilings, mirrors, candelabra, palms and cherubs provides the perfect backdrop for an impressive menu of brasserie-style seafood, roasts, grills and salads, which, although predomi-nantly French, encompasses dishes from around the world. Hugely popular, with a lively pre-dinner bar, La Stampa is always buzzy and good fun.

➕ 185 D3 ⊠ 35 Dawson Street, D2 ☎ 01 677 8611 ⏰ Daily 6pm–midnight

Thornton's €€€

The restaurant of Kevin Thornton, acknowledged as Ireland's finest chef, boasts two Michelin stars. The dining-room is pleasingly understated and the food refresh-ingly simple – an exquisite blend of traditional Irish and southern French cuisine – with heavenly desserts.

➕ 184 C3 ⊠ Fitzwilliam Hotel (▶ 40–41), St Stephen's Green, D2 ☎ 01 478 7008 ⏰ Tue–Sat 12:30–1:45, 7–9:30

Wagamama €–€€

This slick, stylish noodle bar is a Mecca for Japanese food junkies. It serves cheap, tasty rice and noodle dishes in a minimalist basement environment, with long wooden benches and disposable chopsticks, and is currently extremely popular. The gigantic bowls of ramen noodles are a meal in themselves. There's a no-smok-ing policy and no advanced booking, so be prepared to wait to be seated.

➕ 184 C3 ⊠ King Street South, D2 ☎ 01 478 2152 ⏰ Mon–Sat noon–11, Sun noon–10

PUBS

For general pub opening times ▶ 44.

(See also **Pub Crawl**, ▶ 159–161).

Davy Byrne's €

Even though the modern interior is a disappointment, this is one of Dublin's landmark pubs, with its fair share of notable customers over the years: revolutionary Michael Collins, Sinn Féin leader Arthur Griffith, writers Brendan Behan and Liam O'Flaherty and artist William Orpen all drank here, and you can even still follow in the footsteps of Leopold Bloom, James Joyce's protagonist in the novel *Ulysses*, who dropped into the "moral pub" at lunchtime for a gorgonzola cheese sandwich and a glass of burgundy.

➕ 185 D3 ⊠ 21 Duke Street, D2 ☎ 01 677 5217

Doheny & Nesbitt €

This cosy, old-fashioned Victorian pub is just around the corner from An Dáil Éireann (the Irish Parliament) and, as a consequence, has always attracted a vivid cross-section of Dublin society, most notably lawyers, politicians,

Where to...
Shop

If it's smart shopping you're after, Southside East offers the city's best retail selection. Grafton Street, the capital's premier shopping street, is a shopper's heaven, brimming with international designer stores and abuzz with window-shoppers and street musicians from morning till night. Grafton Street also has the nearest thing to a daily *passeggiata*, or promenade, west of Italy, underlining the city's increasingly cosmopolitan atmosphere, as locals promenade and admire each other.

In nearby Nassau Street, bordering Trinity College, a concentration of touristy gift shops conceals one or two real gems offering the finest of Irish handicrafts and knitwear, including the huge Kilkenny Shop. There are plenty more home-styling shops in the area and a wide choice of bookstores near the university for fans of Irish literature. Head further east, away from the frenetic pace of Grafton Street, and you'll find the Georgian quarter dotted with specialist boutiques and many of the old family-owned shops that make shopping in Dublin such a pleasurable experience.

FASHION

You'll be spoilt for choice on and around Grafton Street. There's everything here from major British high-street chains (Next, Jigsaw, Warehouse, Monsoon, Marks & Spencer...) to trendy British boutiques. Try **Pamela Scott** (84 Grafton Street, tel: 01 679 6655) for

---

financiers and journalists. The bar is magnificent – antique and made of mahogany, and there are plenty of wooden partitions for privacy, plus soft lighting. For your second pint, **Toner's** opposite (at No 139, tel: 01 676 3090) is another Dublin institution – an authentic Victorian pub complete with original mirrors, lamps and snug, and old-fashioned drawers once used for storing tea and groceries, especially porter.

🚩 185 E2 ✉ 5 Baggot Street Lower, D2 ☎ 01 676 2945

Kehoe's €

Kehoe's counts among Dublin's most popular, unspoilt old-style pubs, with its original wooden interior of finely carved partitions subdividing the long bar, a cosy snug at one end and a small, intimate lounge at the other. A true city-centre gem, with good beer and great craic.

🚩 185 D3 ✉ 9 Anne Street South, D2 ☎ 01 677 8312

McDaid's €

Once the "local" of Brendan Behan, Flann O'Brien and Patrick Kavanagh, this great literary pub beside the Westbury Hotel draws an eclectic crowd of tourists, bookish types and young Dubliners to its cosy wood and stained-glass interior. On Wednesday and Sunday nights there is sometimes live music from the resident blues band.

🚩 185 off D3 ✉ 3 Harry Street, D2 ☎ 01 679 4395

Mulligan's €

They say that Mulligan's, established in 1782, serves one of the best pints in town. This reputation draws a well-mixed clientele (with very few tourists) and the ban on mobile phones within the pub walls means you can concentrate on the drinking and chat to some local Dublin characters. And, like the porter, the conversation here is always solid, strong and good.

🚩 185 D4 ✉ 8 Poolbeg Street, D2 ☎ 01 677 5582

party kit and cool daywear; **A-wear** (Grafton Street, tel: 01 872 4644), a fashion institution for Dubliners of both sexes; **Ave Maria** (38 Clarendon Street, tel: 01 671 8229), with its sexy line in cocktail dresses and over-the-top jewellery; **Richard Alan's** smart boutique (53 South King Street, tel: 01 677 5149) for exclusively Irish fashions; and **Alias Tom** (Duke Lane, tel: 01 671 5443) for stylish men hooked on such European and American labels as Dolce & Gabbana, Paul Smith, Issey Miyake and Prada.

Grafton Street also boasts a glut of smart shoe shops: **Fitzpatricks** (76 Grafton Street, tel: 01 677 2333) offers ultra-stylish shoes for both sexes; **Carl Scarpa's** small, exclusive boutique (25 Grafton Street, tel: 01 677 7846) is filled with trendy Italian boots and shoes; **Korky's** (47 Grafton Street, tel: 01 670 7943) sells funky shoes for trend-setting shoppers; while **Zerep** (57 Grafton Street, tel: 01 677 8320) is even more wacky and adventurous.

DEPARTMENT STORES

The jewel in Grafton Street's crown is undoubtedly **Brown Thomas** (88 Grafton Street, tel: 01 605 6666), Dublin's most glamorous department store, fantastic for chic fashion separates, international labels, local fashion talent, hats, shoes, linen, lingerie and cosmetics.

BT2 (28–29 Grafton Street, tel: 01 605 6666), its sidekick across the street, appeals to a younger label-conscious age group, with a top reputation for unisex designer sportswear, jeans and casual wear by Tommy Hilfiger, Calvin Klein, Prada Sport, DKNY and others.

At the far end of Grafton Street, the popular **St Stephen's Green** multi-storey mall contains a large **Dunnes Store** (tel: 01 478 0188), the Irish equivalent of Marks & Spencer, with branches throughout the city and the suburbs.

THINGS IRISH

The **Kilkenny Shop** (5–6 Nassau Street, tel: 01 677 7066), at the forefront of contemporary Irish design, is among the best shops in town for stylish gifts and souvenirs. Here you'll find a dazzling choice of local fashions, pottery, jewellery, linen, arts and handicrafts to suit all tastes and budgets, from chunky Aran sweaters and traditional oak walking-sticks to the latest John Rocha Waterford crystal designs.

House of Ireland (37 Nassau Street, tel: 01 671 1111) has a wide selection of woollens, Celtic jewellery and Waterford crystal. A stone's throw away, the name of **Kevin & Howlin** (31 Nassau Street, tel: 01 677 0257), the long-established family firm, is synonymous in Dublin with hand-woven Donegal tweed. It has a splendid range of jackets, waistcoats and the type of suits George Bernard Shaw used to wear, and such classic caps as The Great Gatsby, The Sherlock Holmes, The Quiet Man and The Dubliner. Nearby, **Celtic Note** (14–15 Nassau Street, tel: 01 670 4157) is Ireland's largest traditional music store, offering everything from pub songs and ballads to instrumental collections and Riverdance (▶ 27).

Off Nassau Street, the family-owned and run **Avoca Hand-weavers** company (11–13 Suffolk Street, tel: 01 677 4215, and also at Powerscourt House, Enniskerry, ▶ 146) produces genuine Irish products with an arty twist. Their large city-centre store is a treasure-trove of Irish fashion, crafts, toys and gifts topped by a wonderful café (▶ 109). The studio of **Louis Mulcahy**, Ireland's pre-eminent potter (46 Dawson Street, tel: 01 670 9311), is a must for ceramics collectors. His unfussy designs are beguiling, his luminous glazes

Where to...
Be Entertained

THEATRE & CLASSICAL MUSIC

The **Gaiety** (5 King Street South, D2, tel: 01 677 1717) is the main theatre in this part of town, staging predominantly mainstream productions, especially those of Irish playwrights, but also musicals, ballet, opera and pantomime. After hours, this jewel of Victorian architecture, with its sumptuous gilt, chandeliers and red velvet, opens its doors as a hugely successful late-night club. The auditorium is used to screen old black-and-white movies, while the rest of the premises (three floors and five bars) hosts themed live-music nights of salsa (Fridays), jazz, soul, and rhythm and blues (Saturdays) for a lively party crowd.

Given Dublin's strong musical pedigree, it's hardly surprising

there's a top-notch classical music scene. It is centred on the **National Concert Hall** (Earlsfort Terrace, D2, tel: 01 417 0077), home to the National Symphony Orchestra, which plays there every Friday from November to May, and also offers a programme of opera, chamber music, jazz and dance.

BARS, PUBS & LIVE MUSIC

Needless to say, Dublin's trendy Southside has more than its fair share of chic, stylish bars. Here you can pose with the likes of Eddie Irvine and Jacques Villeneuve in **Samsara** (Dawson Street, D2, tel: 01 671 7723), Bono and The Corrs in **Scarsons** (Baggot Street, D2, tel: 01 660 0330), or join the beautiful people who crowd the street-side

---

adorning everything from tableware to vast signature floor vases.

For up-to-the-minute streamline furniture and accessories, try **Minima** (35 St Stephen's Green, tel: 01 662 7894); the **Apollo Gallery** (51 Dawson Street, tel: 01 670 9528) is great for modern Irish art; and you can't beat the shop at the **National Museum of Ireland** (tel: 01 677 7444; ▶ 97–99) for traditional Irish jewellery designs.

BOOKS

For special editions from leading Irish writers, try the antiquarian bookshop **Cathach Books** (10 Duke Street, tel: 01 671 8676).

Hodges Figgis, near the university (56–58 Dawson Street, tel: 01 677 4754), specialises in Irish literature and academic publications. It also has a good range of tourist guides, general fiction, children's books and an in-store coffee shop.

Murder Ink (15 Dawson Street, tel: 01 677 7570) is a must for

thrillers, mysteries and detective stories, while bargain hunters can stock up at **Greene's** (16 Clare Street, tel: 01 676 2554), an old-fashioned, second-hand specialist and a cult Dublin address.

FOOD

Tiny **Sheridan's Cheesemongers** (11 Anne Street South, tel: 01 679 3143) stocks smoked salmon and charcuterie, and a huge range of locally produced artisan cheeses. The following travel well: Doolin, Carrigaline, Cooleeney Camembert, Knockalara and Brodie's Boilie (preserved in oil).

Dunne & Crescenzi (14 Frederick Street South, tel: 01 677 3815) are the experts on Italian artisan food; and **Butler's Irish Chocolates** (51a Grafton Street, tel: 01 671 0599) has a delicious pick-and-choose selection of gleaming foil-wrapped truffles, with such exotic flavours as tiramisu, apple pie, Baileys...even Guinness!

terrace of the **Bailey** (2 Duke Street, D2, tel: 01 670 4939) and the cavernous *belle époque* **Café En Seine** (40 Dawson Street, tel: 01 677 4567), with its high glass ceilings, palms and mirrors after work.

Older professional types head for the Shelbourne's classic **Horseshoe Bar** (St Stephen's Green, D2, tel: 01 663 4500; ▶112) near An Dáil Éireann (Irish Parliament) for the low-down on the Irish political scene.

The more traditional minded can search for the perfect pint of *Guinness* and a bit of *craic agus ceol* (fun and music) at **O'Donoghue's** (15 Merrion Row, D2, tel: 01 676 2807), where the famous ballad group The Dubliners began their musical career in the early 1960s, and where impromptu sessions are still a regular feature of the pub.

Enter **Kehoe's** (9 Anne Street South, D2, tel: 01 677 8312; ▶113) late at night, and you'll find a smoky atmosphere, raised glasses and lively conversation – overwhelming proof that traditional Dublin pubs are still very much at the heart of the city's social scene.

McDaid's (3 Harry Street, D2, tel: 01 679 4395; ▶113) was in turn a morgue, a Moravian chapel and the local boozer of three major Irish writers – Behan, Donleavy and Kavanagh. Today it still attracts a crowd of serious drinkers but, unlike many of the historic pubs, it plays pop music, with a free blues session every Wednesday and Sunday night.

NIGHTCLUBS

The Southside East area abounds in lively nightspots, including the hugely popular **PoD** (Place of Dance, 35 Harcourt Street, D2, tel: 01 661 0700), a veritable dance emporium with celebrity DJs and on-the-pulse sounds. It is located in the former Harcourt Street railway station. Friday nights play host to HAM at the PoD, where the gay scene enjoys some of the best dance music in town. Also here, and sharing the same quirky buildings, you'll find the ultracool **Odeon** bar and grill (tel: 01 478 2088), the late-night **Lobby Bar** (tel: 01 661 0700), where the jetset start their weekends, and the trendy **Tripod** (tel: 01 661 0700), another venue at the cutting edge of techno and dance music with occasional live performances. Beware of the strict door policy and be prepared to wait for admittance.

Another venue with a strict door policy is **Lillie's Bordello** (Adam Court, Grafton Street, D2, tel: 01 679 9204), a long-established favourite nightclub catering for more mainstream dance sounds and attracting an older clientele. It is popular with visiting musicians, film stars and celebrities and, together with Spirit (▶140) and the PoD, is very much a place to see and be seen.

If your preference is more for chart music, **Major Tom's** (King Street South, D2, tel: 01 478 3266) is a popular disco playing a strong mix of music from the last three decades of the 20th century for a young crowd, while **Renards** (35–37 South Frederick Street, D2, tel: 01 677 5876) offers a varied mix of music on three floors, including frequent live jazz and blues.

Also popular on the Dublin night scene is **The Sugar Club** (8 Lower Leeson Street, D2, tel: 01 678 7188), an exclusive club in a converted cinema, which marks the return of cocktail culture to the capital, and plays live swing, jazz, salsa and blues into the small hours.

Also in Leeson Street, you'll find a handful of basement bars, several of which remain open till around 3 am. The drinks aren't cheap, but if you're still thirsty, they will serve you the latest "last orders" in Dublin.

Northside

Getting Your Bearings

Northside (north of the Liffey) was the last part of the city to be developed, during the 18th century. Although considered less fashionable than Southside, it none the less boasts O'Connell Street, the widest and longest thoroughfare; the tallest building; some of the finest, most fashionable Georgian houses; and such majestic edifices as Gandon's splendid Four Courts and Custom House, both situated along the north Liffey quays and regarded by many as the city's most beautiful buildings.

Above: Early morning in Phoenix Park

The main Northside sights embrace all that is typical of Dublin's culture – story-telling, literature, drama, dance, song, even drinking at the Old Jameson Distillery – all the elements that lead to mighty good *craic*. Dublin boasts a star-studded cast of writers and the Dublin Writers Museum and the James Joyce Cultural Centre, both on the Northside, are dedicated primarily to writers who spent most of their lives here. Ireland's two most celebrated theatres – the Abbey and the Gate – keep the Irish theatre tradition alive, while the thriving music scene, both traditional and modern, flourishes in pubs and The Point.

Previous page: O'Connell Street – the city's main artery

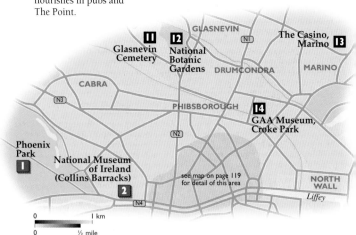

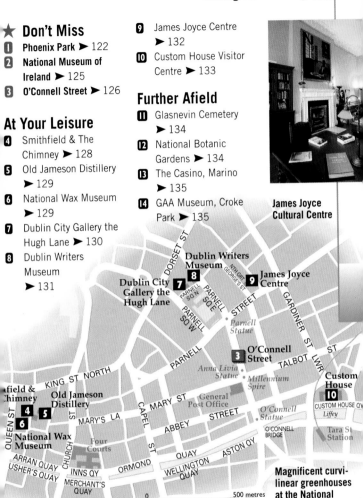

James Joyce Cultural Centre

Magnificent curvilinear greenhouses at the National Botanic Gardens

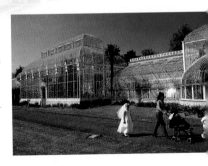

Throughout the area, there is a characteristic mixture of the old with the new: Smithfield market and the dockland area have been rejuvenated; pedestrianisation is creating new spaces for street events; new shops, theatres, museums and entertainment centres have sprung up. Northside may be a late developer, but there's no denying, it is rapidly catching up with the Southside.

Northside is celebrated for its many cultural aspects, so after a leisurely morning in the park, why not immerse yourself in its pleasures of music, literature, drama, drinking and song?

Northside in a Day

9:00 am

Start the day with a pleasant stroll in 1 **Phoenix Park** (➤ 122–124), one of the largest city parks in the world and home to the president of Ireland. You may spot a couple of deer grazing among the trees or come upon a polo match or a game of hurling in full swing. A visit to **Dublin Zoo** (➤ 124) here is an absolute must for children. (Right: Ashtown Castle in the park.)

11:00 am

A short walk along the Liffey brings you to Collins Barracks, which houses a section of the 2 **National Museum of Ireland** (➤ 125).

12:30 pm

If whiskey is your tipple, take a fascinating tour through the 5 **Old Jameson Distillery** (➤ 129), just off 4 **Smithfield** (➤ 128), Europe's largest cobbled square (left), and round it off with a complimentary glass of the strong stuff. Then climb 60m (200 feet) up 4 **The Chimney** (➤ 128, and yes, there *is* a lift!) to admire the beautiful bird's-eye views.

1:30 pm

Head down the quays to the heart of the little Italian Quarter and Enoteca Delle Langhe (➤ 136) for some tasty antipasti and a nice glass of Italian red.

3:00 pm

Catch bus No 90 from Arran Quay to the southern end of **8 O'Connell Street** (➤ 126–127), then walk up Dublin's main and undeniably impressive thoroughfare, dominated by the **General Post Office** (➤ 127), book-ended by statues of two great Irish leaders, Daniel O'Connell (➤ 24) and Charles Stewart Parnell (➤ 54 and 123). Pass the millennium *Spire of Dublin* (above), and the statue of James Joyce (on the corner with Earl Street), then continue on to Parnell Square with its graceful Georgian mansions.

3:30 pm

Explore Dublin's extraordinary literary past at the **8 Dublin Writers Museum** (right; ➤ 131), where all the city's best-known writers – Joyce, Shaw, Stoker, Yeats, Beckett and Behan to name but a few – are documented.

5:00 pm

Have a drink in a pub. In Ireland, you always go to the pub before or after going anywhere else. Conway's (➤ 137) on Parnell Street and The Flowing Tide (➤ 140), nearer the Liffey, are both popular venues for a sundowner. Then, inspired by the city's numerous literary heroes, take in a show at Ireland's national theatre, the Abbey (➤ 139) or, equally famous, the Gate (➤ 139).

10:30 pm

Time for a nightcap? Keating's (➤ 140) is a good choice north of the river, with its established reputation for excellent live traditional music.

Phoenix Park

Phoenix Park is one of the most magnificent city parks in Europe. Laid out in the mid-17th century, it is the green lung of Dublin – a vast expanse of woodland, lakes, hillocks, streams, monuments, formal gardens and ponds in the city centre – and a popular haunt of Dubliners seeking respite from the congestion of urban life.

At 707ha (1,750 acres), Phoenix Park is Europe's largest enclosed city park, five times the size of London's Hyde Park and double the size of Central Park in New York. It was created in 1663, following instructions from King Charles II "to enclose with a stone wall the lands of our ancient inheritance…and to store with deer". It was presented to the City of Dublin in 1745 for use as a public park. Today, the boundary wall is a staggering 11km (7 miles) long, with eight gates for vehicles and six pedestrian entrances, and the park still contains around 500 deer.

There is a lively and entertaining exhibition on the history of the park and its wildlife at the **visitor centre**, including an audio-visual presentation on Phoenix Park through the Ages and a special children's section where youngsters can explore the wonders of forest

Dublin's green lung

🞤 182 A5

✉ Phoenix Park, D7 🚌 Bus 10 (from O'Connell Street), 25, 26, 37 (from Abbey Street Middle)

Dublin Zoo
☎ 01 474 8900; www.dublinzoo.ie 🕐 May–Sep Mon–Sat 9:30–6, Sun 10:30–6; Oct–Apr Mon–Sat 9:30–dusk, Sun 10:30–dusk (last admission 1 hour before closing). Entry to Ashtown Castle and Áras an Uachtarain by guided tour only 💰 Expensive

Visitor Centre
☎ 01 677 0095 🕐 Mid- to end Mar daily 10–5:30; Apr–Sep 10–6; Oct 10–5; Nov to mid-Mar Sat and Sun only 10–5. Áras an Uachtaráin: free guided tours every Sat 10:30–4:30 on the hour (tickets from visitor centre) 💰 (Including Ashdown Castle) inexpensive

fe. Adjoining the centre is the long-hidden **Ashtown Castle**, a medieval tower-ouse that had been incorporated within a modern house. It was only "rediscov-red" in the 1980s when the later addition was demolished due to dry rot. When ne deer park was laid out for King Charles II, the castle passed to a keeper vhose job it was to "prevent the spoil and embezzlement of the vert or the veni-on". Nowadays you can visit both the castle and its miniature maze.

ports

hoenix Park has long been a popular sporting ground, and it's a common sight o see joggers, children practising hurling skills, horse-riders, or a friendly game f Gaelic football being played on the rough open ground. Also within the park s a motor-racing circuit where, in the 1920s, Grand Prix races were held; Nine Acres, the home to the Irish Polo Club (with games most Wednesday, Saturday

The Notorious Phoenix Park Murders

On 6 May, 1882, Lord Cavendish, the Chief Secretary in Ireland, and Thomas Burke, the Under Secretary, were stabbed to death in the park, and the name of Charles Stewart Parnell, leader of the Irish Home Rule Party, was put forward as prime suspect in an attempt to ruin his political career. Back in England, the assassination caused a furore in Westminster, and the question of Home Rule for Ireland was seriously debated. It was later revealed that the brutal knifings were committed by a secret society called the Invincibles, a radical Nationalist movement.

and Sunday afternoons from May to September); and Phoenix Cricket Club, founded in 1830 and the oldest cricket club in the country.

Áras an Uachtaráin

Among the park's impressive mansions is the official residence of the American ambassador to Ireland, Áras an Uachtaráin (the President's Residence). This regal house, bearing an uncanny resemblance to the White House in Washington, was built in 1751 and started life as a glorified park-keeper's residence. It was later remodelled by Frances Johnston, the architect of the neo-classical General Post Office (► 127), and for years housed various British viceroys. Following the establishment of the Irish Free State, it became home to the Governor General and eventually, in 1937, the official residence of the first Irish President, Dr Douglas Hyde. The house is open to the public on Saturdays.

Dublin Zoo

One of Phoenix Park's biggest draws is Dublin Zoo. When it was founded in 1830, its only occupant was a solitary wild boar – hard to believe as you stroll around today's 24ha (60 acres) of landscaped grounds with its 700-plus animals and tropical birds from all corners of the world, many of which are rare or endangered species. Most of the animals were either born in captivity or orphaned in the wild where they faced an uncertain future, and many – including the snow leopards, gorillas and golden lion tamarinds – are part of a global plan to preserve and protect these rare animals. Be sure to visit the World of Cats, Monkey Island, Fringes of the Arctic and the African Plains, and keep the kids amused on the zoo train or at the petting farm. You can watch the animals being fed during the daily Meet the Keeper programme, and visit the Discovery Centre to learn more about the animals, and the zoo's successful breeding and conservation programmes. The original MGM lion was filmed at Dublin Zoo.

What's In A Name
Curiously, the park is not named after the mythical bird, but rather it is said to derive from the Gaelic *fionn uisce*, meaning "clear water", referring to a spring in the Furry Glen, near the Phoenix Column which, to add confusion, is topped by a statue of a phoenix!

TAKING A BREAK

The **Fionn Uisce** restaurant in the grounds of the visitor centre is good for lunch, and the **Phoenix Park tea rooms** are well placed outside the zoo for snacks, coffees and teas but, on sunny days, it's hard to beat a picnic.

PHOENIX PARK: INSIDE INFO

Top tips Allow an hour to visit the visitor centre and Ashtown Castle, and a good couple of hours to visit the zoo.
• The park's **deer** are best spotted around Fifteen Acres, a wide expanse of grassland, and Oldtown Wood, one of the largest woodland areas.

Hidden gem The only cultivated part of the park is the **People's Garden**, a Victorian-style garden with an attractive pond.

In more depth The **Wellington Testimonial** is a 63m (207-foot) obelisk of Wicklow granite with bronze bas-reliefs made from captured French cannon depicting scenes from the Duke's battles.
• The **Papal Cross** was erected to commemorate the mass conducted here by Pope John Paul II to more than a million people in September 1979.

2 National Museum of Ireland (Collins Barracks)

Housed in two wings of the austere and impressive Collins Barracks, the National Museum of Decorative Arts and History provides a vivid and fascinating insight into Ireland's economic, social, political and military progress through the centuries. The dazzling collection comprises around 2,500 precious artefacts ranging from weaponry, furniture, folk-life items and costume to silver, ceramics and glassware. It forms part of the National Museum of Ireland collection together with the National Museum (▶ 97–99) and the Natural History Museum (▶ 108).

Don't miss the **Curator's Choice Exhibition**, where 25 objects chosen by the curators of the various collections are on display. These include a 2,000-year-old Japanese ceremonial bell, the ornate Fleetwood Cabinet presented by Oliver Cromwell to his daughter on her marriage to General Fleetwood, Lord Deputy of Ireland, the gauntlets worn by King William at the Battle of the Boyne (▶ 150), and a 15th-century hurling ball made of hair, traditionally presented by young girls as a token of affection to the hurlers to bring them luck in their May Day contests. Highlights of the other collections include the Fonthill vase, one of the earliest documented pieces of Chinese porcelain; 19th-century neo-Celtic furniture; charming Irish country furniture, and The Way We Wore, depicting 250 years of fashion.

Collins Barracks itself could be described as the National Museum's largest artefact. Commissioned as the Royal Barracks by William III in 1704, it was able to accommodate 5,000 troops. It was renamed in memory of the Republican hero Michael Collins (▶ 25) following Irish independence.

TAKING A BREAK
Soup Dragon (▶ 137) for an exotic selection of home-made soups.

🚇 183 E4 ✉ Collins Barracks, Benburb Street, D7 ☎ 01 677 7444; www.museum.ie
🕐 Tue–Sat 10–5, Sun 2–5 🚌 Bus 25, 25A, 66, 67, 90; free shuttle bus to the National Museum of Ireland, Kildare Street and the Natural History Museum, Merrion Street 🎟 Free

❸ O'Connell Street

The ghosts of Dublin's past are everywhere in the city, but perhaps nowhere more so than on O'Connell Street, with its monuments and historic public buildings. What's more, this impressive, tree-lined boulevard – the widest in Ireland – marks the very centre of the city.

Important figures

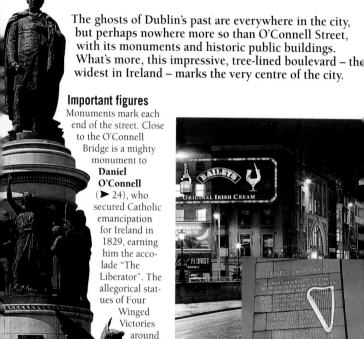

Monuments mark each end of the street. Close to the O'Connell Bridge is a mighty monument to **Daniel O'Connell** (► 24), who secured Catholic emancipation for Ireland in 1829, earning him the accolade "The Liberator". The allegorical statues of Four Winged Victories around the base symbolise O'Connell's qualities of Courage, Fidelity, Eloquence and Patriotism, while the figures around the pedestal represent

Above: Monument to freedom fighter Daniel O'Connell

Right (inset): The Parnell Monument

members of the Church, the professions, the arts and the labouring classes, and Erin, holding up the Act of Emancipation. (The figure of Erin represents the sovereignty of Ireland; the name Eire is a derivative of her name.) When the monument was erected in 1882, the street was officially called Sackville Street. The name change to O'Connell Street took place in 1924, three years after Ireland gained independence.

The northern end of O'Connell Street is marked by a monument to **Charles Stewart Parnell** (► 123), the late 19th-century leader of the struggle for Irish Home Rule. **Parnell Square** beyond, laid out in 1755, was the city's second Georgian square after St Stephen's Green (► 100–104). Today its elegant

Notable O'Connell Street Sculptures

The statue of James Larkin (► 24) depicts the great 19th-century trade unionist in full flow, championing the workers' rights. His fundamental message appears on the plinth: "The great appear great because we are on our knees. Let us arise."

The 120m (400-foot) *Spire of Dublin* is seven times the height of the GPO opposite. Its tip is illuminated from a light source within to provide a beacon in the night sky.

buildings contain Dublin City Gallery the Hugh Lane (► 130–131), the Dublin Writers Museum (► 131–132), the Rotonda Maternity Hospital – the oldest maternity hospital in the world – and the Gate Theatre (► 139). At the centre of the square, the Garden of Remembrance (► 22) is dedicated to those who gave their lives for Irish independence.

The Easter Rising

City developments in the 1960s and '70s left little of Dublin's Georgian architecture standing on O'Connell Street. The grandest building – the Palladian-style **General Post Office**

(GPO) – was the headquarters of the Irish Volunteers during the Easter Rising of 1916. From its steps, Pádraic Pearse (► 25) proclaimed Ireland's independence from Britain and the birth of the Republic, but a week later the Rising had been crushed. Inside is a pictorial account of the Rising, and a small sculpture of Cú Chulainn (► 25), the mythical symbol of Irish heroism.

Above: The General Post Office – scene of the notorious Easter Rising

➕ 184 C5 ✉ O'Connell Street, D1 🚌 Most cross-city buses; LUAS Abbey Street

---

O'CONNELL STREET: INSIDE INFO

Top tip O'Connell Street offers some of the best **shopping** north of the Liffey (► 138–139).

Hidden gems O'Connell Bridge has the unusual distinction of being broader than it is long. It also affords impressive city vistas.
• **Number 42** is the last remaining Georgian house on the street, now part of the Royal Dublin Hotel.

At Your Leisure

sold their wares. Corn and seed brokers abounded, and cattle and potato stores dotted the streetscape. Smithfield retained its place as Dublin's main market until the late 1800s. On the first Sunday of each month, it still hosts a long-established horse market – not thoroughbreds, but rather a more rural spectacle of scruffy ponies and mules with young children riding them bareback over the cobblestones while adults negotiate the price.

Smithfield has undergone a major face-lift. It now has a smart new retail and cultural centre dominated by the Old Jameson Distillery (► opposite) and The Chimney. Towering above the square, this 67m (220-foot) refurbished red-brick distillery chimney, with its two-tier glass observation deck and glass-walled lift, affords breathtaking 360-degree views of the city's skyline from the Wicklow Mountains to Dublin Bay and from Howth to Bray

⁴ Smithfield & The Chimney

Smithfield Square is the largest cobbled square in Europe. Originally laid out in the mid-17th century as a cattle marketplace, for centuries the area was a bustling place of business where traders and merchants

✚ 184 A4 ✉ Smithfield Square, D7
☎ Chimney: 01 817 3800;
www.smithfieldvillage.com 🕐 Mon–Sat
10–5:30, Sun 10:30–5:30 🚌 Bus 25, 25A,
67, 67A (from Abbey Street Middle) 68, 69,
79 (from Aston Quay), 90 (from Connolly,
Tara and Heuston Stations); LUAS
Smithfield 🎫 Moderate

5 Old Jameson Distillery

Think Dublin, think *Guinness*. Yet the city has an equally venerable tradition of whiskey production. Jameson whiskey has been distilled here since 1780 and, although this particular distillery is no longer in use, you can relive the past at the atmospheric visitor centre.

The visit includes a short film called *Uisce Beatha* (The Water of Life) on the history of Irish whiskey, from the 6th century to the present day. This is followed by a guided tour around a detailed reconstruction of the old working distillery to see the unique art of Irish whiskey-making.

Jameson stills (above) and the bottling line (bottom left)

The tour culminates in the Jameson bar, where you will be given a chance to compare Irish whiskey with Scotch and Bourbon. Irish whiskey is unique in the whisky world (note spelling; only Irish whiskey has the "e") because it is distilled three times. This provides the pure, smooth, distinctive taste that distinguishes it from Scotch and Bourbon (many whiskys are distilled only once, Scotch is distilled twice). What's more, Jameson is not only the highest-selling Irish whiskey in the world, but also the fastest-growing spirit brand.

🚹 184 A4 ✉ Bow Street, Smithfield, D7 ☎ 01 807 2355; www.irish-whiskey-trail.com ⏰ Daily 9:30–6 🚌 Bus 67, 67A, 68, 69, 79, 90; LUAS Smithfield 💶 Expensive

6 National Wax Museum

Now housed in the heart of Smithfield, Dublin's answer to Madame Tussaud's is huge fun, especially for children. The main part of the museum concentrates primarily on the people and events which shaped Ireland's history, with life-size figures of such luminaries as Robert Emmet, James Joyce and the Taoisaigh, while the Hall of the Megastars focuses on the world of pop with everyone from Madonna to Michael Jackson, not forgetting Dublin's very own U2. Film buffs will enjoy coming face to face with Yoda, Darth Maul, Anakin Skywalker and Qui-Gon Jinn in the

A Who's Who of Irish Pop

Some names associated with Irish pop: Altan, Ash, Bob Geldof and the Boomtown Rats, Boyzone, The Chieftains, Chris de Burgh, Christy Moore, The Clancy Brothers, Clannad, The Corrs, The Cranberries, The Dubliners, Hothouse Flowers, Mary Black, Plantxy, Phil Coulter, The Pogues, Rory Gallagher, Ronan Keating, Sinead O'Connor, Stiff Little Fingers, Thin Lizzy, The Thrills, U2, The Undertones, Van Morrison, Westlife...No wonder Dublin was dubbed "City of a Thousand Bands" when the film *The Commitments* premièred here in 1991.

museum's latest exhibit, Star Wars, while the Chamber of Horrors with its demons and surprise shocks is only for the very brave! For younger children there are also puppet shows four times daily.

➕ 184 A4 ✉ Smithfield Square, D7 ☎ 01 872 6340 🕐 Mon–Sat 10–5:30, Sun noon–5:30 🚌 Bus 67, 67A, 68, 69, 79, 90; LUAS Smithfield 💶 Expensive

7 Dublin City Gallery the Hugh Lane

The Municipal Gallery of Modern Art is situated in Charlemont House, one of Dublin's finest Georgian buildings. Formerly a town house owned by Lord Charlemont, a con-

The reconstruction of Francis Bacon's studio

noisseur and patron of the arts, it was first opened to the public in 1930 to display the treasured Impressionist paintings of collector Sir Hugh Lane.

The entrance hall contains some noteworthy 20th-century Irish installation work, including Patrick O'Reilly's *Wringer*, and *Monkey and Dog* by John Kindness, depicting the sectarian conflict in Northern Ireland by use of simile, with "a menacing Republican dog locked in combat with a conceited Orange monkey". Beyond, the sculpture gallery exhibits works by Rodin, Epstein, Degas and Moore. The next gallery contains a fine collection of paintings by Dublin-born "impressionists", Jack B Yeats, William Leech, Walter Osborne and others. Hugh Lane's French Impressionist paintings hang in a small room to the left of the sculpture gallery, and include Claude Monet's *Waterloo Bridge* and Renoir's celebrated *Les Parapluies*.

The gallery recently received the gift of the entire studio of Francis Bacon at 7 Reece Mews, London from Bacon's sole heir, John Edwards. The Francis Bacon Studio – his work and living space for the last 30 years of his life – has been reconstructed, together with an audio-visual room documenting the removal and reconstruction process. The museum stages temporary exhibitions on the first floor. There is also a café and gift shop.

The Hugh Lane expanded to allow a more substantial exhibition of the permanent collection as well as providing specially designed galleries for

Above: Inside
the Dublin
Writers
Museum
Left: Brendan
Behan's typewriter

W B Yeats, Samuel
Beckett, Flan
O'Brien, Brendan
Behan and many
others – are fea-
tured, together with
letters, manuscripts,
photographs, rare
books, paintings,
personal belongings
and other memora-
bilia. Of particular
note are Oliver

the
temporary exhi-
bition programme.
There is also an education
resource room and lectures facility.

🔳 179 F1 ✉ Charlemont House,
Parnell Square North, D1 ☎ 01 874
1903; www.hughlane.ie ⏰ Tue–Thu
9:30–6, Fri–Sat 9:30–5, Sun 11–5
🚌 Bus 3, 10, 11, 11B, 13, 16, 19
💶 Expensive

🎱 Dublin Writers Museum

This museum is a must for anyone
who is interested in Dublin's immense
literary heritage. Ireland has produced
a surprising number of the world's
greatest writers and here, inside a
beautiful 18th-century town house,
all the best-known writers of the city
– Jonathan Swift, George Bernard
Shaw, Bram Stoker, James Joyce,

Off The Beaten Track
A visit to **St Michan's Church** (open
Mar–Oct Mon–Fri 10–12:30, 2–4:30,
Sat 10–12:45; Nov–Feb Mon–Fri
12:30–3:30, Sat 10–12:45) is only for
the brave, for in the crypt of this church
lie the mummified remains of John &
Henry Sheares, Barristers of Law,
executed for their part in the Irish
Rebellion of 1798. The guide provides
the full gory account of what happened
to them!

St John Gogarty's flying goggles; James Joyce's animal-embroidered waistcoat; portrait photographs of Oscar Wilde and Samuel Beckett by the sea; and such celebrated first editions as *Ulysses*, *The Dubliners* and *Dracula*.

The museum often holds exhibitions and readings and has a special room devoted to children's literature. There is also a library of rare books, a gallery of portraits and busts, a Zen garden, a bookshop and a café.

➕ 179 F1 ✉ 18–19 Parnell Square North, D1 ☎ 01 872 2077 ⏰ Mon–Sat 10–5 (also 5–6, Jun–Aug), Sun 11–5 🚌 Bus 10, 11, 11B, 13, 13A, 16, 19, 19A 💷 Expensive

🔵 James Joyce Centre

More than any other Irish writer, it was James Joyce (1882–1941) who celebrated the character of the

Ulysses **mural at the James Joyce Centre**

Joyce's Dublin

Much of Joyce's Dublin still survives and fans of Leopold Bloom, the hero of *Ulysses*, can retrace his footsteps around the city on 16 June, 1904, with the assistance of the Ulysses Map of Dublin (available from Dublin Tourism, ➤ 37). Bloom's lunchtime route through the city centre is marked by a series of 14 bronze pavement plaques, running from the Evening Telegraph Office in Prince's Street to the National Museum (➤ 97–99).

capital in his work and this centre, housed in a beautifully restored Georgian town house, is dedicated to his life and literary masterpieces. Among manuscripts and various items of memorabilia is a fascinating set of biographies of around 50 characters from Joyce's most famous novel, *Ulysses*, all based on real Dublin people. You can also watch short films on Joyce and his Dublin, and listen to recordings of the great master reading from his works. The centre organises walking tours of Joyce's Dublin (➤ panel above) and, in the courtyard of the centre, a striking mural based on the novel and the door of No 7 Eccles Street – the fictional home of Leopold and Molly Bloom.

➕ 180 A1 ✉ 35 Great George's Street North, D1 ☎ 01 878 8547; www.jamesjoyce.ie ⏰ Tue–Sat 10–5 🚌 Bus 3, 10, 11, 13, 16, 19, 22, 123; LUAS Connolly Station 💷 Moderate

dome, took ten years to build and has survived a somewhat varied history.

Gandon's first obstacle was the marshy ground alongside the Liffey. This he overcame with an innovative form of raft foundation, which brought him international acclaim. His second problem was the threatening letters he received from opponents of the scheme. As a consequence, he always carried a sword when visiting the building site. In 1789 a mysterious fire damaged the partially completed edifice, then there was another in 1833. Major catastrophe struck during the War of Independence, when the IRA torched it in 1921. Restored in time for its

⑩ Custom House Visitor Centre

The Custom House, designed by James Gandon (1743–1823) to replace the old customs point further up the River Liffey, is considered by many to be the most magnificent building in Dublin. This beautifully proportioned Georgian masterpiece,

Gandon's Custom House

with its portico of Doric columns and a dazzling 38m (125-foot) copper

bicentenary in 1991, it now houses a visitor centre recounting the history of the Custom House and an account of Gandon's life and work in Ireland.

From the outside, the best view of the Custom House is from George's Quay, on the opposite side of the river. Note the arms of Ireland crowning the two pavilions and a series of 14 allegorical heads depicting Ireland's main rivers and the Atlantic Ocean. Atop the copper dome, the statue of Commerce commands one of the best views of the Liffey.

For Kids

Dublin Zoo (➤ 124)
GAA Museum, Croke Park (➤ 135)
National Wax Museum
(➤ 129–130)
The Bram Stoker Dracula Experience
(West Wood Club, Clontarf Road, D3, tel: 01 805 7824, open Fri 4–10pm, Sat and Sun noon–10pm; ➤ 12) – the spine-chilling interactive tour (every hour on the hour) is brilliant for older children (aged 13 and above).

🚩 185 E5 ✉ Custom House Quay, D1
☎ 01 888 2538 🕐 Mid-Mar to Oct
Mon–Fri 10–12:30, Sat–Sun 2–5; Nov to
mid-Mar Wed–Fri 10–noon, Sun 2–5
🚆 Tara Street DART Station
💶 Inexpensive

Further Afield

11 Glasnevin Cemetery

Celtic cross

Glasnevin Cemetery opened in 1832, primarily to allow Catholics a place of burial following the abolition of the Penal Laws in 1829.

Today, 4km (2.5 miles) from the city centre, on 49 landscaped hectares (121 acres), the cemetery has grown to become a national institution. It is Ireland's largest graveyard, and the final resting place of more than a million men, women and children. From the tragic paupers' graves of the famine and cholera victims of the 1840s to ornately carved Celtic crosses, elaborate Gothic mausoleums and the tombs of such notables as Daniel O'Connell (➤ 24), Michael Collins (➤ 66), Eámon de Valera (➤ 25), Charles Stewart Parnell (➤ 123), William Butler Yeats (➤ 13) and Brendan Behan (➤ 13), this peaceful corner of Dublin reflects the social, political and cultural history of the last two centuries.

🚹 179 D5 ✉ Finglas Road, Glasnevin, D11 ☎ 01 830 1133; www.glasnevin-cemetery.ie/ 🕐 Mon–Sat 8–4:30, Sun 9–4:30. Guided tours start from the main gate, Wed and Fri 2:30–4:30 🚌 Bus 13, 19, 19A (from O'Connell Street to Harts Corner plus 5 minutes' walk), 40, 40A (from Parnell Street to Finglas Road) 🎫 Free

12 National Botanic Gardens

Established in 1795, the National Botanic Gardens are the country's premier centre of botany and horticulture, but to most Dubliners they are simply a popular weekend destination for a gentle stroll amid the 20,000 different species of flora found here. Highlights include the glorious herbaceous displays; the Victorian carpet bedding; the bog, Burren and vegetable gardens; the renowned rose garden; the yew walk and an arboretum containing hundreds of tall specimen trees – something to please the botanist, gardener and casual visitor alike.

Late spring and summer are the best seasons to visit, but even during winter there is plenty to see, thanks to the dazzling displays in the magnificent curvilinear cast-iron glasshouses, built

Inside the Palm House

in 1843 by the Dublin iron-master Richard Turner. Here you will find banana trees, bamboo, huge Amazonian creepers, orchids, cacti, a rare collection of cycads and, in the Aquatic House, the amazing giant Amazonian water lilies.

🔲 179 D5 ✉ Glasnevin, D11 ☎ 01 857 0909 🕐 Mon–Sat 9–6, Sun 10–6, in summer; Mon–Sun 10–4:30, in winter. Glasshouses open restricted hours 🚌 Bus 13, 19 (from O'Connell Street), 134 (from Middle Abbey Street) to Botanic Road 🎫 Free

🅱 The Casino, Marino

This charming little villa in the suburb of Marino, just 5km (3 miles) north of the city centre, is considered among Dublin's most intriguing buildings, and one of the finest examples of Palladian architecture in Ireland – full of quirky design foibles, including hollow columns to accommodate drainpipes and chimneys disguised as urns. The Casino (meaning "small house") was designed by Sir William Chambers in the 1760s as a bachelor pad for Lord Charlemont, and contains 16 finely decorated rooms. Entry is by guided tour only.

🔲 181 F5 ✉ Off the Malahide road, Marino, D3 ☎ 01 833 1618; www.heritageireland.ie 🕐 Feb, Mar, Nov and Dec Sun and Thu noon–4; Apr

The Casino, Marino

Sat–Sun noon–5; May and Oct daily 10–5; Jun–Sep daily 10–6 🚌 Bus 20A, 20B, 27, 27B, 42, 42C (from city centre near Busaras), 123 (from O'Connell Street); Clontarf Road DART Station 🎫 Inexpensive

🅲 GAA Museum, Croke Park

This state-of-the-art interactive museum under the stands at Croke Park, the headquarters of the Gaelic Athletic Association (GAA), provides an insight into Ireland's unique national games: hurling and Gaelic football. Amid trophies, colourful kits and ancient hurlers (hurling sticks), the ground floor follows the chronological story of the games, while the links with the nation's history are powerfully told in film. Upstairs, try your luck at interactive kicking or pucking, or test your athletic reflexes and watch thrilling excerpts from some of the classic All-Ireland hurling and football finals. With so much to see and do, allow a match-long period for your visit!

🔲 180 B2 ✉ Croke Park, D3 (entrance under the Cusack Stand, via Clonliffe Road) ☎ 01 819 2323; www.gaa.ie 🕐 Mon–Sat 9:30–5, Sun noon–5 (except Sun match days when the museum is open to stand ticket-holders only, noon–3) 🚌 Bus 3, 11, 16, 51A, 123 🎫 Moderate

Bloody Sunday

Dublin has often witnessed the conflicting cultural and political traditions of Ireland reflected on the playing field. The worst instance was on Bloody Sunday, 21 November, 1920. That morning, on the orders of Michael Collins, the IRA murdered 12 Englishmen suspected of being intelligence agents. Later that day, a Gaelic football match between Dublin and Tipperary was scheduled at Croke Park, with the proceeds going towards arms for the Irish Volunteers. Just 15 minutes before play, a combined body of Black & Tans (the British auxiliary police force, then employed in Ireland against the republicans) and Dublin Metropolitan Police entered the stadium and began firing indiscriminately. Twelve people were killed including Tipperary rugby back Michael Hogan, after whom the present Hogan Stand is named, and a further 60 injured.

Where to...
Eat and Drink

Prices
Expect to pay per person for a three-course meal, excluding drinks but including VAT
€ under €30   €€ €30–50   €€€ over €50

The Northside of Dublin (north of the River Liffey) does not have the number or variety of restaurants you'll find elsewhere in the city, though there are several worth a special journey, as well as some excellent cafés and pubs.

RESTAURANTS & CAFÉS

Chapter One Restaurant and Café €€
This stylish restaurant serves modern Irish cuisine in a series of brightly coloured interconnecting dining rooms within the arched basement of the Dublin Writers' Museum, near the Gate and Abbey theatres. Original stonework, mirrors, drapes and paintings of literary celebrities add to the ambience. By day the restaurant is full of local business clientele. By night, the two-course pre-theatre menu is especially popular, and the service is obliging – dessert and coffee can be completed after the performance.

🚪 179 F1 ✉ 18–19 Parnell Square, D1 ☎ 01 873 2266 🕐 Tue–Fri 12:30–2:30, 6–11, Sat 6–11

Condotti €€
A trendy, modern pasta restaurant – part of the popular British Pizza Express chain – Condotti serves tasty, affordable versions of well-known favourites as well as more unusual pasta combinations, with plenty of choice for vegetarians. An open kitchen adds to the fun atmosphere, and there's a tiny terrace for alfresco dining, plus a comfortable lounge area for drinks and coffee.

🚪 184 C4 ✉ 38 Ormond Quay Lower, D1 ☎ 01 872 0003 🕐 Mon–Sat noon–midnight, Sun noon–11:30

Enoteca Delle Langhe €–€€
The newly developed "Quartier Bloom" (a tribute to Joyce's most famous character) is a little Italian quarter on Ormond Quay with a few casual eateries around a communal plaza area dominated by a mural with a very modern take on The Last Supper. Delle Langhe is at the heart of the quarter, with an authentic *enoteca* experience of affordable Italian wines and tasty selection of antipasti. But it's the laid-back atmosphere that really sets this place apart, perfect for summertime people watching.

🚪 184 C4 ✉ Blooms Lane, D1 ☎ 01 888 0834 🕐 Mon–Sat 12:30–11

Halo €€€
This split-level restaurant in the Morrison Hotel (▶ 42), designed by John Rocha with velvet throws, dramatic spot lighting and clean crisp lines, is currently the trendiest dining-room in town. The imaginative menu of exciting Asian-influenced fusion food is perfectly complemented by the relaxed yet impeccable service, making dining here a truly memorable experience. Judges from the nearby Four Courts can often be seen here enjoying a house special such as the monkfish Wellington.

🚪 184 C4 ✉ Morrison Hotel, Ormond Quay Lower, D1 ☎ 01 878 2400 🕐 Daily 12:30–2:30, 7–10:30

The Old Jameson Distillery €

The restored Old Jameson Distillery is a great place for a hearty, Irish-style lunch. The bright, modern café-style **Still Room Restaurant** serves such wholesome specialities as bacon and cabbage soup and John Jameson casserole. Or, for something lighter, the distillery bar – the **Irish Whiskey Corner** – dating from 1780, serves soup and sandwiches, with wines, beers and more than 14 different whiskeys.

✚ 184 A4 ☒ Bow Street, D7
☎ 01 872 5566 ⊙ Daily 9–5:30

101 Talbot €

A friendly, first-floor restaurant near the Abbey and Gate theatres and especially popular with theatre-goers, 101 Talbot serves hearty, wholesome meat and fish dishes and an imaginative choice of vegetarian dishes too. The simple decor is enlivened by displays of contemporary art for sale.

✚ 185 D5 ☒ 101 Talbot Street, D1
☎ 01 874 5011 ⊙ Tue–Sat 5–11

Soup Dragon €

Tiny it may be, but Soup Dragon dishes up a splendid and varied menu of fresh soups in three sizes. Good choices include Thai chicken and hearty mussel, potato and leek. They also specialize in delicious smoothies and a mean cup of coffee. The cost of soup includes some homemade bread and a piece of fruit for dessert.

✚ 184 B4 ☒ 168 Capel Street North, D1 ☎ 872 3277 ⊙ Mon–Fri 9–5:30, Sat 11–5

The Vaults €€

This long neglected, beautiful space underneath Connolly train station was developed into a restaurant in 2002 and was an instant hit. Cavernous arches and smooth Portland stone floors set the elegant tone and it's a great spot for a pre-dinner cocktail. The Italian chef makes everything on the premises, including fantastic pizzas and mouth-watering ice cream. Note that dinner is only served until 8,

when it becomes a bar and club until late.

✚ 180 C1 ☒ Harbourmaster Place, D1 ☎ 01 605 4700 ⊙ Daily noon–8

The Winding Stair €

Native Dubliners complained when the old bookstore/café of the same name closed its doors, but the new, buzzing eatery that took its place has silenced every critic. Overlooking the Ha'penny Bridge, the food is simple, no-fuss high-quality Irish cuisine with the bacon and cabbage always a big favourite.

✚ 184 C4 ☒ 40 Ormond Quay Lower, D1 ☎ 01 872 7230 ⊙ Daily 12:30–10:30

PUBS

For general pub opening times ▲ 44.
(See also **Pub Crawl**, 159–161)

Conway's €

Founded in 1745 and showcased in the film *The Commitments* (▲ 11),

this timeless, comfortable pub is a true Dublin classic, serving up good pub food and superbly creamy *Guinness* to a daily crowd of locals and performers from the nearby Gate Theatre.

✚ 184 C5 ☒ 70 Parnell Street, D1
☎ 01 873 2474

The Gravediggers €

Not only does this sixth-generation, family-run, old-style pub (one of several in Dublin known as Kavanagh's) have a wonderful, almost countrified atmosphere, it also serves one of the cheapest pints in town and is well worth the bus or taxi ride from the city centre. Located at the gates of Glasnevin Cemetery (▲ 134), its nickname hails from the days when the muddy workmen digging the graves would slide a shovel through a hatch in the back wall of the pub as a tray to be filled with pints of *Guinness*.

✚ 179 E4 ☒ Prospect Square, Glasnevin, D9 ☎ No phone

Where to... Shop

Shopping north of the Liffey offers a truly authentic Dublin experience, and is more suited to good-value standard shopping than the more individual and sophisticated Southside boutiques.

The main shopping area here is always densely crowded with Dubs rather than tourists. It extends from O'Connell Street, the city's main drag, along pedestrianised Henry Street to Capel Street and is dominated by department stores and high-street retailers such as Marks & Spencer, Debenhams and Next. Just off Henry Street, the Monday-to-Saturday Moore Street fruit, flower and vegetable market provides a taste of trading as it was here in

bygone days, where some pedlars still unload their wares from horse-drawn carts and call out their prices in old Dublin dialects. The chances are that horses may not be on your shopping list, but on the first Sunday of each month, Smithfield Square stages a long-established horse market (▶ 128). The Smithfield area has long been a famous trading centre and was Dublin's main market venue from the Middle Ages until the late 1800s. Now the area has been rejuvenated and a new shopping centre brimming with traditional Irish crafts has been created on the site of an old medieval walkway called Duck Lane.

DEPARTMENT STORES

Apart from **Brown Thomas** (▶ 114), you'll find most of Ireland's top department stores here. Some, including **Arnotts** in Henry Street (tel: 01 805 0400) and **Clery's** (tel: 01 878 6000), with its well-stocked Irish gift section, in

O'Connell Street Lower, are unique to Dublin. Clery's is Dublin's original to Dublin. Clery's is a little more chic, specializing in quality but conservative women's clothing, and also has a floor of home appliances and interior design items. Arnotts is Ireland's oldest and largest department store, full of affordable fashions and children's wear with good beauty, interiors and sports departments too. Also on Henry Street, **Roches Stores** (tel: 01 873 0044) is especially popular with locals, with five floors of fashions, while **Debenhams** in Jervis Street (tel: 01 878 1222) is popular for interiors as well as clothing. International designer John Rocha has recently joined forces with Debenhams to create five exclusive collections – women's, men's and children's wear, accessories, and home – all at high-street prices. The store forms part of the massive, modern **Jervis Street Shopping Centre** (tel: 01 878 1323), Dublin's largest mall. **Pennies** (tel: 01 872 0046) on Abbey Street is beloved of thrifty

Dublin housewives. It's a good spot for disposable, fun fashion. The **Ilac Centre** is Dublin's original shopping mall with entrances along Henry Street.

THINGS IRISH

More Street off Mary Street is something of a Dublin institution where women sell fruit and vegetables from their carts and are famed for their sharp, biting wit. Stallholders also sell shoes and boots and other bric-à-brac. Immigrant traders have joined in to give the place a wonderful "one-world" vibe.

For jewellery, **McDowell** (3 O'Connell Street Upper, D1, tel: 01 874 4961) specialises in traditional hand-crafted gold and silverware. Celtic metalwork was once the pride of Ireland and many crafts-people are still inspired by the traditional designs found on ancient chalices and ornaments. The most famous design of all is probably the

Where to...
Be Entertained

Claddagh ring – the lovers' symbol of two hands cradling a heart and a crown.

A picture of Dublin makes a memorable souvenir of your visit. Take a look in the **Davis Gallery** (11 Capel Street, D1, tel: 01 872 6969) at their choice selection of original paintings and water-colours by Irish artists, or the **Irish Historical Picture Company** (5 Ormond Quay Lower, D1, tel: 01 872 0144), for old Irish photographs. **Ha'Penny Bridge Galleries** (15 Bachelors Walk, D1, tel: 01 872 3950) is a lovely, intimate antiques shop with four floors of Irish curios, including bronzes, silver and pottery.

BOOKS

Eason and Son (40 O'Connell Street, tel: 01 858 3800) is the biggest bookseller in town, with a wide range of Irish literature and national and international newspapers. **Connolly Books** (Bloom

Lane, D1, 01 874 7981) is Dublin's only political bookstore and is well known for its section on Irish History and feminism.

MUSIC

Nearly all the top music shops are north of the river, including **Waltons** (2–5 Frederick Street North, D1, tel: 01 878 3131) and **Goodwins** (134 Capel Street, D1, tel: 01 873 0846), who both sell fine hand-crafted *bodhrán* drums (▶ 26), handmade harps, *uilleán* pipes and other traditional instruments.

FOOD

Dublin foodies head to the **Moore Street Market** (▶ 138), and to the **Epicurean Food Hall** (Liffey Street Lower), with its galaxy of food specialists from around the world. Nearby, **Australian Homemade**'s (41 Abbey Street Upper, D1) too-good-to-eat designer Belgian chocolates are a chocoholic's dream.

THEATRE

The north side of the Liffey boasts Dublin's two most celebrated theatres. Critics rate the works performed at the **Gate Theatre** (Cavendish Row, D1, tel: box office 01 874 4045) as the best in Ireland. Founded in 1929, it is best known for its modern Irish plays and its contemporary interpretations of popular international plays, while its great rival, the **Abbey Theatre** (Abbey Street, D1, tel: box office 01 878 7222), is internationally renowned for its productions of older Irish plays by such authors as Brendan Behan, Sean O'Casey, George Bernard Shaw and William Butler Yeats. The Abbey's smaller **Peacock Theatre** downstairs

focuses on more experimental, avant-garde works, providing a platform for work by emerging Irish talent.

CINEMA

The film *The Commitments* (based on the best-selling book by the popular contemporary novelist and Dubliner, Roddy Doyle, ▶ 12), premiered at the **Savoy Cinema** (17–18 O'Connell Street Upper, D1, tel: 01 874 6000) on 19 September, 1991, renewing local interest in movies. Now Ireland has the largest cinema-going audience per capita in Europe with the huge **Cineworld** (Parnell Street, D1, tel: 1520 880 444) as one of the main cinemas in Dublin town.

COMEDY

Although Dubliners have long enjoyed a reputation for being witty, entertaining folk with a fondness for joking and story-telling, professional stand-up comedy is a relatively new phenomenon. Pubs are the most popular venues for impromptu sessions. Comedy lovers need look no further than the Laughter Lounge (4–6 Eden Quay, D1, tel: 01 878 3003) for a feast of local and international stand-up talent from Thursday to Saturday. Performances start at 9pm and advance booking is advised. Murphy's has now reopened after a major renovation.

PUBS & LIVE MUSIC

Although there are fewer pubs north of the Liffey than on Southside, there are nevertheless some absolute corkers. **The Flowing Tide** (9 Abbey Street Lower, D1, tel: 01 874 4108), for instance, situated diagonally opposite the Abbey Theatre, is a popular watering-hole for the post-theatre crowd, and every inch of the pub is covered in old and new theatrical posters. Long-established **Slattery's** (129 Capel Street, D1, tel: 01 872 7971) and **Keating's** (9–10 Jervis Street, D1, tel: 01 873 1567) are two of Dublin's top venues for traditional live music sessions.

The nearby **Cobblestone Bar** (77 King Street North, Smithfield Square, D7, tel: 01 872 1799) is the heart of traditional music in the Smithfield area, with some of the country's top session players turning up for impromptu gigs. The atmosphere is intense, but always welcoming. Further afield, the Irish music sessions at the 16th-century **Abbey Tavern** in the seaside suburb of Howth (tel: 01 839 0307; ▶ 164–166) are a Dublin institution. **GUBU** (Capel Street, D1, tel: 01 874 0710) is one of the city's most popular gay bars, but the loud dance-driven music and the down-

stairs pool table attract a sizeable straight crowd.

TRENDY BARS

Northside boasts some of the most stylish bars in town. The pricey **Morrison's** bar in Dublin's Morrison Hotel (Ormond Quay Lower, D1, tel: 01 887 2400; ▶ 42) is a top people-watching venue with sexy people and sexy staff in sexy surroundings, created by John Rocha, Ireland's leading designer. And zany **Lobo**, the bar downstairs, is just impossibly cool.

At **Zanzibar** (34–5 Ormond Quay Lower, D1, tel: 01 878 7212), you are transported to an exotic land full of palm trees at the city's largest and most over-the-top theme bar, a veritable drinking emporium on the banks of the Liffey with loud music and large crowds.

Equally popular **Pravda** (2–3 Liffey Street Lower, D1, tel: 01 874 0090), once a lost-property office, is now a modern, chic enclave of

sophistication filled with striking communist iconography.

The Dice Bar (79 Queen Street, D7, tel: 01 674 6710) in Smithfield, is a real music-lover's dive, with DJs spinning electronic sets most nights.

CONCERT VENUES

Spirit nightclub (formerly the celebrated concert venue HQ; 57 Abbey Street Middle, D1, tel: box office 01 884 3633), hosts a variety of local and international acts including David Bowie, Suzanne Vega, Van Morrison, Nina Simone and Westlife to name but a few.

The Point (East Link Toll Bridge, North Wall, D1, tel: box office 01 836 3633) is Dublin's premier concert venue, a huge concert hall developed from former dockland warehouses that also stages major rock events and such box-office blockbusters as Riverdance. The Point even has its own heli-pad for the pop stars.

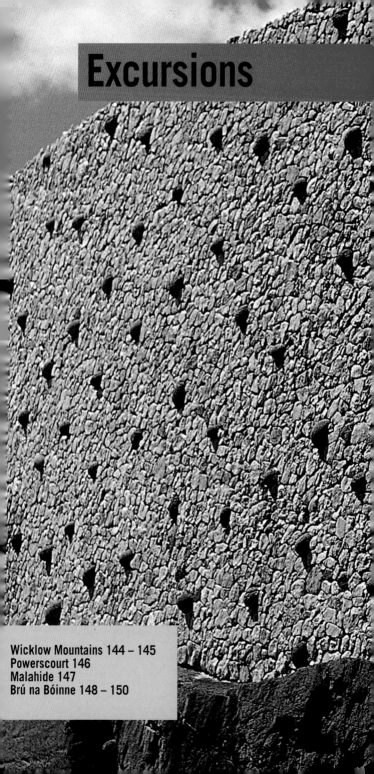

Excursions

Excursions

Just a short distance outside Dublin, the beautiful Irish countryside offers a wealth of attractions ranging from dramatic mountains and ancient Celtic burial sites to stately homes and pretty seaside villages. Most of the sights are within an hour's drive of the city and make ideal day and half-day excursions.

The counties immediately surrounding Dublin constitute the "Pale", the area of Ireland most strongly influenced in the past by English rule. Consequently, they are exceedingly rich in history, and brimming with abbeys, castles, churches and some of the country's finest stately homes. North of Dublin, in County Meath, the fascinating ancient passage tombs at Newgrange (► 148–149) are Ireland's most remarkable neolithic treasures. They are situated in the Boyne Valley, another popular destination for those tracing Irish history and the famous battle fought here (► 150) which resulted in a landmark Protestant victory over the Catholics – foretelling of England's involvement in Ireland's politics.

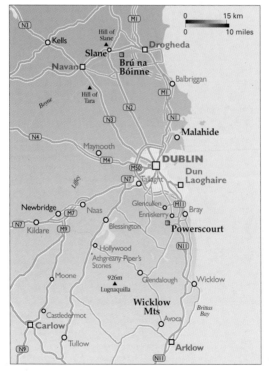

Top right: Glendalough, at the heart of the Wicklow Mountains

Page 141: Detail of a passage tomb at Brú na Bóinne

Closer to Dublin, head to the seaside for a fun day out. The coastline both north and south of Dublin is dotted with picturesque fishing villages, attractive towns, magnificent sweeping sandy beaches and rugged cliff-top walks, and provides plenty of opportunities for yachting, sailing, windsurfing and fishing. Two of County Dublin's most popular coastal villages are especially easy to reach by DART (➤ 38): picturesque Howth is beloved by locals and visitors alike for its seafood restaurants and breezy headland (➤ 164–166), while Malahide (➤ 147) is best known for its medieval castle and its lively bars and pubs. To the south, the coastline is most spectacular beyond Bray, with Brittas Bay in County Wicklow boasting the best beach.

The capital's immediate hinterland is County Kildare, and the heart of Ireland's celebrated horse-racing country. The National Stud at Tully (➤ 33), founded by an eccentric Anglo-Irish colonel in 1900, is well worth a visit to watch the horses being exercised and groomed.

Perhaps the most popular excursion from Dublin is to the heather moors and wooded glens of the Wicklow Mountains (➤ 144–145). Not only is this empty, rugged expanse of beautiful, untamed countryside a walkers' paradise, it is also home to some of the region's most impressive sights, including the evocative settlement of Glendalough, one of Ireland's most venerated monasteries (➤ 144), and the elegant gardens of Powerscourt House (➤ 146).

Getting around

The best way to explore the lush, green countryside around Dublin is by car, although the DART north–south rail link provides easy access to many coastal suburbs. Alternatively, enjoy the countryside at a leisurely pace on a bicycle, or sit back and enjoy an organised tour. **Bus Éireann** (tel: 01 836 6111), **Wild Coach Tours** (tel: 01 280 1899) and **Gray Line Tours** (tel: 01 670 8822) all offer full day tours to Newgrange and to the Wicklow mountains; **Dublin Bus** (tel: 01 873 4222) arranges half-day coach tours of the north coast (including Malahide and Howth) and the south coast (including Killiney, Bray, Avoca and the Wicklow Mountains).

For something more energetic, consider walking the Wicklow Way with **South West Walks Ireland** (tel: 066 712 8733) or a cycling weekend tour from Dublin to the Wicklow Mountains with **Irish Cycling Safaris** (tel: 01 260 0749).

Megalithic art at Newgrange

Wicklow Mountains

These rugged hills on Dublin's doorstep represent all that is best about the wild Irish landscape, with their lush glens, broad lakes and waterfalls, remote blanket bogs, bleak heather-clad heaths and dramatic peaks. Little wonder the Wicklow Mountains are one of the capital's favourite green lungs, filling the skyline to the south and enticing city-dwellers out at weekends to visit the "Garden of Ireland".

No other capital city in Europe lives so close to a mountain range of such great size, variety and beauty as Dublin, with spectacular walks and views which begin just 17km (11 miles) south of the city centre. Although the Wicklow peaks are small compared to the great mountain ranges of the world, they are high by Irish standards: **Lugnaquilla**, at 926m (3,038 feet), is the country's third highest peak.

The main roads from Dublin into the Wicklow Mountains (via the Sally Gap, the Wicklow Gap or over Powerscourt Mountain) all offer striking viewpoints, but the real pleasure of this region is to go off the beaten track and explore the more remote corners of County Wicklow for yourself.

Glendalough

The area's main attraction is Glendalough – a ruined monastic settlement founded in the 6th century by the great misogynist and ascetic St Kevin, a member of the royal house of Leinster who became a recluse of the early Celtic church and built a contemplative cell in this deep, lovely valley in order to

escape the sinful world. The site quickly became a major religious settlement in early Christian Ireland, with a Europe-wide reputation for learning for many centuries, until its final demise following the Reformation in the 16th century.

Today, Glendalough's remains include a perfectly preserved, 12th-century Round Tower (33m/108 feet high), sturdy little chapels, a stone-built oratory and numerous Celtic crosses set against a magnificent mountainous backdrop. There are also two lakes near by – hence the name *Glendalough* (glen of the two lakes) – and a well-maintained forest trail to the top end of the valley, which rewards walkers with memorable views.

Ancient stones

According to folklore, the **Athgreany Piper's Stones** – 14 prehistoric stones in a circle, with another just outside the formation – are the bodies of people turned to stone for dancing on pagan ground. The rock outside the ring is said to be the piper. They are located south of Blessington, on the road between Hollywood and Donard.

TAKING A BREAK

Stop at Ireland's highest pub, **Johnnie Fox's** (tel: 01 295 5647), at Glencullen on the northern rim of the Wicklow Mountains. Undeniably touristy, it's celebrated for its fantastic seafood and traditional music sessions.

Above: Glendalough

Left: The Wicklow Mountains

✉ Glendalough, County Wicklow (signposted from Kilmacanogue) ☎ 0404 45325 ⓘ Visitor Centre: mid-Oct to mid-Mar daily 9:30–5; Sep to mid-Oct/mid-Mar to May 9:30–6; Jun–Aug 9–6:30 🚌 Take the N81 Wexford road south from Dublin. Turn left at Hollywood on to the R756 to Glendalough. Allow a good hour (depending on the traffic) 💷 Visitor centre: moderate. Monastic site: free

---

WICKLOW MOUNTAINS: INSIDE INFO

Top tip Be sure to use a **good map** if you intend to walk in the Wicklow Mountains. Sheets 56 and 62 of the Irish OS 1:500,000 series cover the area in detail.

In more depth The 132km (82-mile) **Wicklow Way** stretches from Dublin over the Wicklow Mountains to Clonegal in County Carlow, starting just outside Dublin in Marlay Park. Contact the Irish Tourist Board for a pamphlet (▶ 170).

Must-see The picture-postcard village of **Avoca** in the southern part of the Wicklow Mountains, better known to the world as "Ballykissangel", is something of a Mecca for fans of the popular television series. The village also contains Ireland's oldest hand-weaving mill, the **Avoca Handweavers**, where you can purchase their beautifully woven fabrics.

Powerscourt

Powerscourt House looks out over an elegant terrace

The gardens at Powerscourt, just 25km (16 miles) south of Dublin, are considered among the finest in Ireland, both for their design and for their magnificent setting in the Wicklow Mountains.

They were first created in the mid-18th century, but redesigned in the 19th century with carefully planned gardens to the south and a series of formal rides and parkland to the north. Sweeping terraces link the house to the main lake and lead the eye onwards to the distinctive slopes of the Sugar Loaf Mountain. The surrounding grounds are a spectacular blend of formal gardens, statuary and ornamental lakes, together with rambling walks, a walled rose garden and a pet cemetery.

The land was granted to the 1st Viscount Powerscourt, Sir Richard Wingfield, by James I in 1609. Wingfield commissioned Richard Castle (1690–1751) to design a magnificent Palladian mansion around the shell of an earlier castle. In 1961 the Slazenger family (of tennis fame) bought the estate from the 9th viscount, and opened the gardens to the public. The house had just been restored when it was burned to a shell in 1974. Only the ballroom and garden rooms have since been restored. The remaining space has since been taken up with craft and design shops, and the popular Terrace Café. The leaflet *A Walk Through Powerscourt Gardens* (at reception) outlines three routes around the grounds.

Powerscourt Waterfall, at 121m (397 feet) the highest in Ireland, is set in romantic landscape 6km (4 miles) by car from Powerscourt Gardens.

✉ **Powerscourt Estate, Enniskerry, County Wicklow** ☎ **01 204 6000; www.powerscourt.ie** ⏰ House & Gardens: 9:30–5:30, Mar–Oct; 9:30 am–dusk rest of year; closed 25 and 26 Dec 🚌 Take the N11 road south from Dublin. Turn off at Enniskerry (south of Bray) and follow signs to Powerscourt 💶 **Expensive**

Malahide

The picturesque seaside village of Malahide is becoming an increasingly fashionable place to live. By the sea, near the airport, and just 14km (9 miles) north of Dublin, it boasts excellent restaurants, lively pubs, chic boutiques, a smart new marina development and Malahide Castle.

Malahide Castle – one of Ireland's oldest castles

The huge and impressive castle stands in a large, wooded demesne. It remained in the hands of the Talbot family from around 1200 until 1976, except for a brief interlude during the rule of Oliver Cromwell (1653–58). A guided tour of the interior enables you to witness the castle's transition over the centuries from a simple medieval fortress to a stately home of fairy-tale appearance, complete with turrets and towers. Most of the furnishings are Georgian, in keeping with the castle's décor, and some of the National Portrait Collection is housed in the castle's grand banqueting hall here, including portraits of various Talbot family members.

The castle grounds provide plenty of opportunity for walking and picnicking, and the **Talbot Botanic Gardens**, created by the late Lord Milo Talbot between 1948 and 1973, are well worth visiting. You'll also find the **Fry Model Railway** here. This huge collection of handmade model trains and trams from the beginning of rail travel to the present day is the largest such display in the world, running on a zero-gauge track through a landscape featuring all the main Dublin landmarks.

Finally, don't miss **Tara's Palace**, a unique dolls' house and toy collection, painstakingly constructed by some of Ireland's finest craftsmen, with miniature paintings by leading Irish artists.

✉ Malahide, County Dublin 🚌 Bus 42 or DART train to Malahide

Castle
☎ 01 846 2184 🕐 Apr–Oct Mon–Sat 10–5, Sun 10–6; Nov–Mar Mon–Sat 11–5, Sun 10–5 💶 Expensive; combined ticket for castle, and Fry Model Railway/Tara's Palace available

Fry Model Railway/Tara's Palace
☎ 01 846 3779 🕐 Apr–Sep Mon–Sat 10–5, Sun 2–6; closed Oct–Mar
💶 Moderate

Brú na Bóinne

The tranquil 15km (9-mile) stretch of lush farmland at Brú na Bóinne (a bend in the Boyne) in County Meath, 53km (33 miles) north of Dublin, marks the cradle of Irish civilisation. Today it boasts Europe's richest concentration of ancient monuments – forts, henges, standing stones and the mysterious grand passage tombs of Newgrange, Dowth and Nowth.

This fertile river valley was first settled during the Stone Age and soon became the most important settlement in the country. The Brú na Bóinne Visitor Centre helps to interpret the neolithic monuments in an extensive exhibition, including a full-scale replica of the chamber at Newgrange and a model of one of the smaller tombs at Knowth.

Newgrange

The spectacular passage grave at Newgrange is, without doubt, the high point of a visit to Brú na Bóinne, staggering for its sheer size and complexity of construction, and containing the greatest concentration of megalithic art in all Europe. This massive, grassy tumulus, measuring 85m (280 feet) in diameter and more than 10m (30 feet) high, dates from around 3000 BC. Its exterior walls are faced with brilliant white quartzite resembling a giant kerbstone. The sophisticated entrance, with its large, mysteriously carved Threshold Stone, is constructed with a narrow slit in the stone like a letterbox. It would seem that the chamber had a significance beyond that of a burial place as, once a year on the morning of the winter solstice, the rays of the sun flood through this slit and illuminate the interior.

A guide leads you by torchlight along a 19m (62-foot) passage to the beehive-shaped central burial chamber, to marvel at the intricate patterns of the wall carvings. When Newgrange

Passage grave, Newgrange

was excavated, only a handful of bodies were found, which was considered unusual given the sheer size of the burial chamber. Nobody really understands why this was, but it would appear that the funerary remains were regularly removed – perhaps once the sun had taken the spirits of the dead with it, following the winter solstice?

Newgrange is just one of around 40 burial sites within this celebrated bend in the Boyne. Nearby are the mounds of Dowth, 3km (2 miles) east of Newgrange (visible from the road); Knowth, 1.5km (1 mile) northwest of Newgrange, with its magnificent megalithic tomb art; and various other strange tumuli, some of which have not yet been excavated.

Slane

It's not just Newgrange that makes the Boyne Valley so cele-brated. Indeed, it was on the nearby Hill of Slane that, in 344, St Patrick is said to have ceremoniously kindled the flame of Irish Christianity. According to legend, the druids were celebrating their feast day on the Hill of Tara, but before they could ignite their sacred fire, Patrick had prepared his Easter feast and had lit his Paschal fire at Slane. The story goes that having seen the flames, the druids warned High King Laegaire that if Patrick's fire were not immediately extinguished, it would burn forever in Ireland!

Battle of the Boyne

The Boyne Valley returned to prominence on 1 July, 1690 at the Battle of the Boyne. Having been deposed from his throne in 1866, the Catholic ex-King of England, James II, rallied his supporters, the French and Irish Catholics, and challenged his successor, the Protestant King William of Orange, at Oldbridge on the banks of the river. A bloody battle ensued. The Protestants triumphed and James fled to France. The battle signalled the start of total Protestant power over Ireland, and the suppression of Catholic interests. Three centuries later the mention of this feud continues to fuel Irish passions – not so much the battle, but what it represents: the continuing differences between Catholics and Protestants, and the difficulty of overcoming the past in search of a common future.

✉ Boyne Valley Archaeological Park, 11km (7 miles) southwest of Drogheda, County Meath
☎ 041 988 0300; www.heritageireland.ie
🕐 Newgrange: Jun to mid-Sep daily 9–7; May 9–6:30; mid- to end Sep 9–6; Mar–Apr, Oct 9:30–5:30; Nov–Feb 9:30–5. Last tour 1.5 hours before closing time. Knowth: May–Oct: visits by conducted tour only
🚌 Take the N1 Belfast road out of Dublin to Drogheda, then follow signs to Brú na Bóinne, south of the River Boyne on the L21
💶 Variable

Hill of Slane

Opposite page: Rowan Gillespie's *Famine Figures*

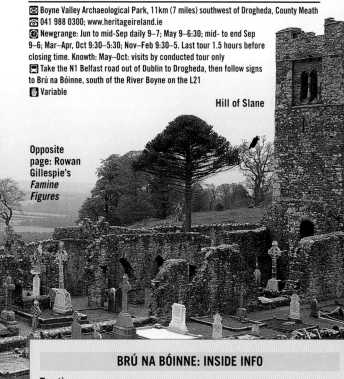

BRÚ NA BÓINNE: INSIDE INFO

Top tips Access to Newgrange and Knowth is by **guided tour only**. If possible, book well in advance. Alternatively, arrive early, book up your guided tour of Newgrange immediately, and be prepared for delays during summer months.
• If you have pre-booked, you are expected to **arrive at the visitor centre at the appointed time**, *not* at the monuments.

Must see The simulated **solstice experience** at the replica Newgrange burial chamber is well worth doing. There is a ten-year waiting list of people wanting to experience the real phenomenon!

Walks & Tours

1 VIKING & MEDIEVAL DUBLIN

Walk

This walk combines Dublin's castle and cathedrals with some of the lesser-known historic sights. It's best done on a Sunday, when there's less traffic and the peal of church bells helps to create a more "medieval" atmosphere.

DISTANCE 3.2km (2 miles)
TIME 1.5 hours
START/END POINT Dublin Castle, Dame Street, D2 ⊞ 184 B3

1–2

Start at **Dublin Castle** (➤ 64–67), the heart of the historic city and the site of the *Dubh Linn* (Black Pool), where the Vikings once moored their longboats. Leave via the main entrance, passing the

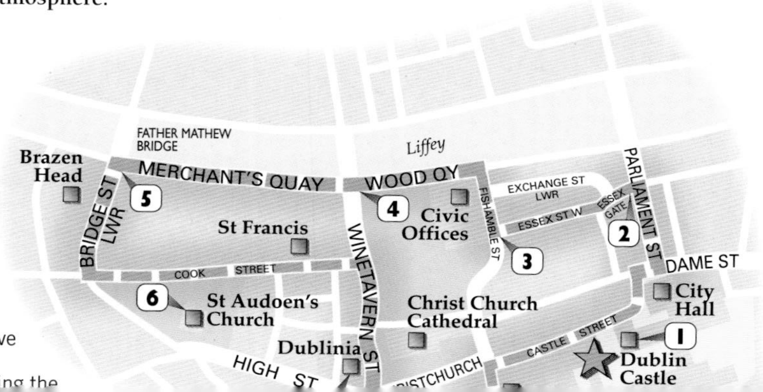

City Hall on your right. Turn right on to the main street. The traffic lights here mark the site of Dame Gate, one of the principal gateways to the walled medieval city, long since

How to get there

Bus 54 (Burgh Quay), 50, 50A, 56A, 77, 77A, 77B (Eden Quay)

Taking a Break

Try **Leo Burdock's** (➤ 77) for the best fish 'n' chips in town.

demolished. Turn left down Parliament Street, then left again into a narrow street called Essex Gate, where a bronze plaque on a stone pillar marks the original site of Essex Gate, another former entrance to medieval Dublin.

2–3

To your right, Exchange Street Lower follows the curve of the walls. It used to be called Blind Quay, because the city walls obscured views of the river. Continue along Essex

Map labels: Liffey, WOOD QUAY, DAME ST, PARLIAMENT ST, EXCHANGE ST LWR, ESSEX GATE, ESSEX ST LWR, FISHAMBLE ST, CASTLE STREET, City Hall, Dublin Castle, Civic Offices, Christ Church Cathedral, WINETAVERN ST, MERCHANT'S QUAY, FATHER MATHEW BRIDGE, St Francis, COOK STREET, Dublinia, St Audoen's Church, HIGH ST, Brazen Head, BRIDGE ST LWR, POSTCHURCH

commemorates the event. From here, head downhill towards the Liffey. Before you turn left into Wood Quay, on your right is Betty Maguire's celebrated *Viking Boat* sculpture. Continue along Wood Quay, past the modern **Civic Offices** (▲ 156) built by Dublin Corporation on top of the old Viking settlement.

4–5

Cross over Winetavern Street and continue down Merchants' Quay to **Father Mathew Bridge**, the site of the fordable crossing that gave Dublin its Irish name, *Baile Átha Cliath* – "Town of the Hurdle Ford".

5–6

Turn left up Bridge Street Lower past Dublin's oldest pub – the **Brazen Head** (▶ 82) – dating from 1198 (although the current building is 17th-century). Turn left again into Cook Street. The large section of fortified wall here is a mainly reconstructed version of the original city wall built around 1100. The street is named after the cooks who had to prepare food outside the city as most of the buildings, and even the walkways, were made of wood and highly inflammable. Halfway along on your

of the ancient lanes here, has been called various names over the centuries, including Stable Lane, Smock Alley and Orange Street. Soon you will reach Fishamble Street.

St Audoen's Gate (▶ 154)

3–4

In the 10th century Fishamble Street was the main thoroughfare from the Viking port to the High Street, the principal trading street. It takes its name from the fish stalls or "shambles" that once lined its streets. In 1742, Handel conducted the première of his *Messiah* in a music hall here, performed by the joint choirs of St Patrick's and Christ Church cathedrals. A plaque at the entrance to the George Frederick Handel Hotel

Map labels:

STEPHEN
200 metres
200 yards
GOLDEN LANE
BRIDE STREET
STREET
Garda Station
8
St Patrick's Cathedral
Marsh's Library
ST PATRICK'S CLOSE
KEVIN ST UPPER
STREET
PATRICK STREET

right, St Audoen's Gate – Dublin's only remaining medieval gateway – leads to **St Audoen's** Protestant church (▲ 70–71), the city's only surviving medieval parish church.

6–7

Continue along Cook Street, past the Church of St Francis on your left. It is more commonly called the "Adam and Eve" church, after a former tavern here that concealed a secret chapel during the days of Penal Law in the 18th century. Turn right up Winetavern Street to **Christ Church Cathedral** (▲ 72), the city's oldest building and the mother church of Dublin. It is joined to **Dublinia** (▲ 71), a museum of medieval Dublin, by a covered bridge, which was added to the cathedral during major reconstruction in the 1870s.

7–8

Cross over the major junction at Christchurch Place, passing the sunken Peace Park and the ruins of St Nicholas "Within" (the city walls). Proceed down Nicholas Street to **St Patrick's Cathedral** (▲ 61–63), founded in 1191 outside the city walls on the site of an earlier wooden church. Notice that the level of its entrance (in St Patrick's Close) is 2m (6 feet) lower than the modern street; it's at the

MARSH'S LIBRARY

8–9

Turn left into Kevin Street Upper. The **Garda Station** on the left here occupies the Episcopal Palace of St Sepulchre, home of the archbishops of Dublin from the late 12th century until 1830 when the Dublin metropolitan police took possession. Turn left into Bride Street, then fourth right into Golden Lane where the façades of some of the buildings incorporate carved scenes from *Gulliver's Travels* (right), in honour of Jonathan Swift, the Dean of St Patrick's (▲ 23 and 62). Take the left fork into Stephen Street Upper, then first left into Ship Street Great, round the back of Dublin Castle, where there is a section of the old city wall.

original level of the medieval city. Halfway up St Patrick's Close is **Marsh's Library** (▲ 75), the oldest public library in Ireland

9–1

Turn right into Werburgh Street. The tall spire of St Werburgh's Church on the right was dismantled in 1810 because the authorities feared snipers might use the site to fire into Dublin Castle. Turn right into Castle Street. From here it's a short walk back to the

2 THE LIFFEY

Walk

DISTANCE 3.2km (2 miles) **TIME** 1.5 hours
START POINT Heuston Station ➕ 183 D3
END POINT Pearce Station ➕ 185 E4

The Liffey has always been Dublin's nerve centre and its main artery, neatly bisecting the city from west to east. To walk along its banks provides a fascinating insight into the city's maritime history, from its Viking origins to the latest modern dockland developments.

1–2

Start at **Heuston Station**, Dublin's most impressive train station, and one of Europe's finest. Named after Seán Heuston, a rebel of the 1916 Easter Rising, the building bears the date 1844, even though a stonemason's strike delayed its completion until 1848. Cross the Liffey to the Northside, over the yellow Frank Sherwin Bridge (1982), and proceed along Wolfe Tone Quay – named after the father of Irish Republicanism (➤ 23), past Collins Barracks (➤ 125) on your left. The **Guinness Brewery** is on the opposite bank. It once had its own jetty here, from which ten

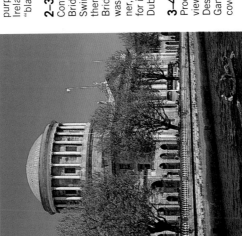

purpose-built Guinness barges set out along Ireland's inland waterways to distribute their "black gold".

2–3

Continue on the north bank past Rory O'More Bridge (1863), the start point for the Liffey Swim (➤ 33), and Mellowes Bridge (1768), then cross over the 1818 Father Mathew Bridge (➤ 153). In Viking times the river here was around 250m (820 feet) wide. On the corner, **O'Shea's Merchant pub** (➤ 82) is celebrated for its live traditional music. Opposite lies Dublin's oldest pub – the **Brazen Head** (➤ 82).

3–4

Proceed along Merchant's Quay, with its grand view of the **Four Courts** on the opposite bank. Designed by English-born architect James Gandon with a Corinthian portico and copper-covered lantern dome, it is considered by many

Gandon's majestic Four Courts

Frieze detail on Sunlight Chambers

to be the finest 18th-century public building in Dublin.

4–5

Pass O'Donovan Rossa Bridge (1816) and the monstrous greenhouse-like **Civic Offices** of the Dublin Corporation on Wood Quay, built in the 1970s and received with dismay by most Dubliners, who dubbed them "the bunkers". On the corner of Essex Quay and Parliament Street stands **Sunlight Chambers**, a turn-of-the-20th-century building with terracotta friezes advertising the company's product – soap. The bridge here was first erected in 1678 by Sir Humphrey Jervis, a nobleman who was developing land on the north side of the river in order to connect his properties advantageously to the castle. It was rebuilt in its present form

in 1753, modelled on Westminster Bridge in London and named Grattan Bridge after Henry Grattan, the formidable leader of the old Irish Parliament. Cross over the bridge, glancing behind you at the magnificent classical façade of the **City Hall** (➤ 72) as you go.

5–6

Continue eastwards along the smart wooden boardwalk, constructed in 2000, which runs parallel to Ormond Quay. The quays on the north bank of the Liffey date mostly from the late 17th century and were laid out in graceful irregularity. These buildings were Dublin's earliest merchant houses, and those along Ormond Quay are particularly attractive. On the opposite bank, the tall narrow houses of Wellington Quay provide an almost continental feel. This was the last city quay to be built, in

Clarence Hotel (➤ 40). Upstream from the Clarence, the River Poddle, the main waterway of medieval Dublin, joins the Liffey through an opening in the quay wall. There was a harbour here until 1625, making Temple Bar Dublin's busiest trading area, and the Clarence was once the Custom House. However, as the average tonnage of vessels increased the docks were forced to move further east.

6–7

The next and newest bridge – the gleaming chrome Millennium Bridge (1999) – is solely pedestrian, linking Northside with Temple Bar. Alongside it, a second pedestrian-only bridge – **Ha'penny Bridge** (1816) – is one of the oldest cast-iron structures of its kind in the world. It derived its popular name from the toll charged to cross it for more than 100 years. Opposite the bridge, look out for the sculpture *Meeting Place* by Jakki McKenna on a bench, nicknamed "The Hags with the Bags".

7–8

O'Connell Bridge (1880) marks the end of the boardwalk and also the finishing line of the Liffey Swim (➤ 33). Continue eastwards past

(▶ 133), the highlight of Dublin's Georgian heritage.

8–9

At the Talbot Memorial Bridge (1978) turn left up Memorial Road and into Amiens Street. Turn first right into the Custom House Docks,

the area that replaced Temple Bar when the new Custom House and its adjoining dock basins were opened in 1791. They, too, were abandoned in the early part of the 20th century – the era of even larger ships – and in 1987 development commenced to rejuvenate the area with the new high-tech Financial

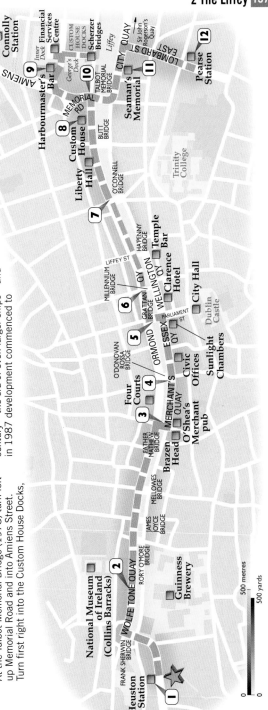

Services Centre. The water resources have been maintained as a central feature of this new district. Walk past the Harbourmaster's Bar, cross a small bridge and turn immediately left to arrive at the Inner Dock, an area of major residential development.

9–10

Return to the bridge, turn left and immediately right on to

George's Dock, where the preserved (but derelict) "Stack A" tobacco warehouse is among the world's finest remaining examples of 19th-century industrial architecture. Head past an antique, hand-operated crane down towards the Liffey and the restored **Scherzer Bridges** (1912), which regulate the entrance to the docks. Look out for the

immense building known as **Liberty Hall**, at 16 storeys the city's sole skyscraper; it's the highest building in Dublin and the second highest in Ireland. To the right of the Scherzer Bridges the moving sculpture group of emaciated figures – *Famine Figures* – by Rowan Gillespie, was created in memory of the Great Famine of 1845–49.

10–11

Return to the Talbot Memorial Bridge, cross the Liffey and continue along City Quay to the **Seaman's Memorial**, a large anchor commemorating the 13 Irish merchant ships and their crews lost in World War II – a high number considering the small fleet and the neutral position of Eire. Beyond lies the deep-water docks and the open sea. Sir John Rogerson's Quay, which runs eastwards from here, was neglected for decades but is now on the verge of a complete redevelopment (overseen by the Dublin Docks Development Authority), incorporating shops, hotels, pubs, restaurants and apartments.

11–12

From the Seaman's Memorial it is a short walk down Lombard Street East to Pearse Station.

Taking a Break

Several pubs and restaurants line the Liffey. Alternatively, try the **Harbourmaster's Bar** at Custom House Docks: the interior re-creates a 19th-century maritime provisions store.

3 PUB CRAWL
Walk

"Good puzzle would be to cross Dublin without passing a pub," mused Leopold Bloom in James Joyce's novel *Ulysses*, and the task proves just as difficult today. Dublin is world famous for its pubs and the city is awash with them. With more than a thousand to choose from, this "crawl" takes you to some of the best – for beer, for atmosphere, for music, for literary associations, for good *craic* (▶ 9).

1–2

Start the pub crawl at **Mulligan's** (▶ 113) in Poolbeg Street. Not only is it among the city's most famous pubs, but it also serves one of the best pints of *Guinness* in Dublin. The interior is rough and ready and usually pretty noisy; the Victorian pub frontage is one of Dublin's finest. To reach it, turn left out of Tara Street DART Station along George's Quay. Take the first left then the first right into Poolbeg Street.

DISTANCE 1.6km (1 mile) **TIME** Depends on your thirst!
START POINT Mulligan's, Poolbeg Street, D2 ✚ 185 D4; get there from Tara Street, DART Station
END POINT Toner's, 139 Baggot Street Lower, D2 ✚ 185 E2

2–3

After Mulligan's, return to the quayside and proceed to the O'Connell Bridge. Turn left down Westmorland Street and right into Fleet Street. The old **Palace Bar** (▶ 81) here was a popular haunt for journalists and writers in the mid-20th century. The front bar is long and narrow, while the back of the pub feels more like a living room than a pub.

3–4

Go further along Fleet Street into Temple Bar where you will be spoilt for choice of watering holes. Try **Oliver St John Gogarty** (▶ 78), the **Temple Bar** (▶ 81) or the **Farrington's** (▶ 81). Continue to Parliament Street where you will find the modern, lively **Porterhouse** (▶ 78), which brews its own porter, ale and lager.

4–5

Head up Parliament Street. Turn left at the traffic lights into Dame Street, first right down

There's often live music at Oliver St John Gogarty's

South Great George's Street, then first into narrow Dame Lane to the **Stag's Head**. This attractive, country-style pub, named after the stuffed and mounted stags' heads on its walls, has original Victorian mirrors, lamps and stained-glass windows, and a magnificent bar topped with red Connemara marble. The lunches here are excellent too.

5–6

Continue to the end of Dame Lane, bear right into Trinity Street, and left into St Andrew Street. Ahead of you on the corner opposite Dublin Tourism is the mock-Tudor, half-timbered façade of **O'Neills**, on the corner of Church Lane and Suffolk Street, one of the most boisterous pubs in the city – a hugely popular student haunt with five bars, just a stone's throw from Trinity College.

6–7

Proceed down Suffolk Street towards Trinity College and turn

Grafton Street. A clutch of good pubs lies just off Grafton Street. In Wicklow Street **The International** and the comfortable **Old Stand** (opposite, in Exchequer Street) are traditional meeting places for rugby fans before an international match. In Duke Street **Bailey's** (▶ 116), with its long literary traditions, vies for custom with

Davy Byrne's (▶ 112), celebrated for its Joycean connections. In Anne Street South there's **Kehoe's** (▶ 113), a genuine old-style pub with traditional décor, intimate surroundings and excellent *craic*, while **McDaid's** (▶ 113) in nearby Harry Street is a must for Behan, O'Brien and Kavanagh fans. **Neary's** (also called the **Chatham Lounge**), just off Grafton Street on Chatham Street, is a popular haunt of actors from the nearby **Gaiety Theatre** (▶ 115). You'll find a comforting atmosphere, a well-worn interior, creamy pints of porter and friendly bar staff there.

7–8

At the end of Grafton Street, turn left along the edge of St

250 metres

250 yards

GEORGE'S QY

Tara Street Station

TARA STREET

Mulligan's
POOLBEG ST

Trinity College

O'CONNELL BRIDGE

WESTMORLAND ST

Palace Bar
FLEET STREET

TEMPLE BAR

Oliver St John Gogarty

CHURCH LA

O'Neill's

SUFFOLK ST

International

WICKLOW STREET

Temple Bar STREET

Norseman
Porterhouse

DAME
DAME LANE

STREET

STH GRT GEORGE'S ST

TRINITY ST ST ANDREW ST

Stag's Head
EXCHEQUER ST

Old

PARLIAMENT STREET

City Hall

Dublin Castle

North then first left up Dawson Street. Almost immediately on your left is the **Dawson Lounge** (No 25), Dublin's smallest pub. Arrive early to get a space at the bar.

8–9

Continue along St Stephen's Green North, past **The Shelbourne Hotel** (➤ 42). A little further down the street, on Merrion Row, you'll find

Nesbitt's (➤ 112) with its fine mahogany bar – a favourite after-work haunt for lawyers, journalists and politicians, but surprisingly devoid of tourists. Nearly opposite, **Toner's** (➤ 113) is another wonderfully traditional 19th-century pub, complete with a snug, ancient mirrors and old-fashioned drawers once used for storing tea and groceries. It is allegedly the only pub Irish writer William Butler Yeats ever entered. Yeats was brought here by his friend, the local surgeon Oliver St John Gogarty, who lived in nearby Ely Place. Yeats sat in the snug just inside the door, politely sipped his sherry, then rose swiftly saying to Gogarty "I have seen a pub now, will you kindly take me home?" Toner's marks the end of the pub crawl.

O'Donoghue's

(➤ 116), Dublin's most famous music pub where the legendary folk group The Dubliners (➤ 26) began their musical career around 40 years ago. If you're lucky, you may find an impromptu traditional music session in full swing.

9–10

Continue straight on into Baggot Street Lower, the location of cosy, antique-style **Doheny &**

4 GEORGIAN DUBLIN

Walk

DISTANCE 2km (1 mile)
TIME 1 hour
START/END POINT St Stephen's Green ⊞ 185 D2; take bus 10, 11, 13, 14, 14A, 15A, 15B

Dublin treasures its Georgian past and this walk, around three of the city's five Georgian squares, highlights some of its finest architecture, as well as drawing attention to the quirkier features of the period.

1–2

St Stephen's Green is one of the landmarks of the Georgian city and **Newman House** (▶ 102), designed in 1739, was the first stone-faced house on the Green. Set off from here, heading eastwards along the south side of the Green, past splendid **Iveagh House** (▶ 103). At the southeastern corner, glance to your right up Earlsfort Terrace to the **National Concert Hall**, Ireland's foremost classical concert venue.

2–3

Cross over and continue straight ahead

left leads to Fitzwilliam Square, the smallest and last of Dublin's five Georgian squares to be completed, but arguably the best preserved, and the only Georgian square whose park is still reserved for residents. Notice the doorways painted in bright colours, and such original details as antiburglar spikes set in the walls.

3–4

Walk around the south and east sides of the square, keeping the park railings on your left, then head up Fitzwilliam Street. This impressive thoroughfare was known as the Georgian Mile as it contained the longest stretch of uninterrupted Georgian town-house architecture in Europe – until the 1960s, that is, when an outrageous piece of civic vandalism allowed the construction of a hideous modern office building to house the Electricity Supply Board. Ironically, that same company has completely restored one of the Georgian mansions, at No 29, converting it into a small museum

4–5

By now you have reached the southeastern corner of **Merrion Square** (▶ 106–107), one of Dublin's grandest squares. To your right is the late Georgian **St Stephen's Church** in Mount Street Upper, fondly known as the Pepperpot because of its unusual dome. In Georgian times, the Grand Canal behind the church would have been a bustling waterway of commerce.

5–6

Turn left along the south side of Merrion Square. Look closely and you will find a wide variety of decorative fanlights, wrought-iron balconies, boot-scrapers, and even coal-hole covers in the street outside each house. At weekends, the railings of Archbishop Ryan Park, in the centre of the square, are hung with hundreds of

Taking a Break

Indulge in a traditional high tea at **The Shelbourne Hotel** (▶ 112) on St Stephen's Green.

(▶ 105–106) and Leinster House, then take the second right into Molesworth Street, where three early Georgian houses with curvaceous gables and huge chimneys are known as the **Dutch Billies.**

8

Turn left down Dawson Street, past **St Ann's Church** (▶ 105) and the attractive Queen Anne-style **Mansion House**, home of the Lord Mayor. Back at St Stephen's Green, turn left and cross Kildare Street to reach **The Shelbourne Hotel** (▶ 42 and 112).

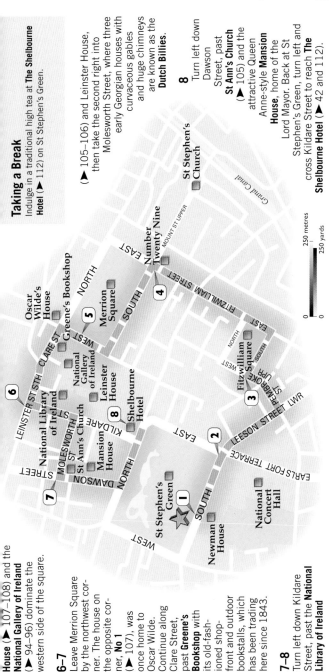

House (▶ 107–108) and the **National Gallery of Ireland** (▶ 94–96) dominate the western side of the square.

6–7

Leave Merrion Square by the northwest corner. The house on the opposite corner, **No 1** (▶ 107), was once home to Oscar Wilde. Continue along Clare Street, past **Greene's Bookshop** with its old-fashioned shopfront and outdoor bookstalls, which has been trading here since 1843.

7–8

Turn left down Kildare Street, past the **National Library of Ireland**

5 HOWTH HEAD
Walk

DISTANCE 11km (7 miles)
TIME Minimum 4 hours
START/END POINT Howth DART Station ✚ 181 off F4

A bracing stroll around the coastal promontory of Howth Head, with its dazzling 360-degree views over the city, Dublin Bay, and the hills and coastline for 50km (30 miles) around is, without doubt, the most spectacular walk on the north side of Dublin. It also provides a perfect respite from the hurly-burly of the city centre.

Getting there

DART train to Howth (24 minutes from the city centre).

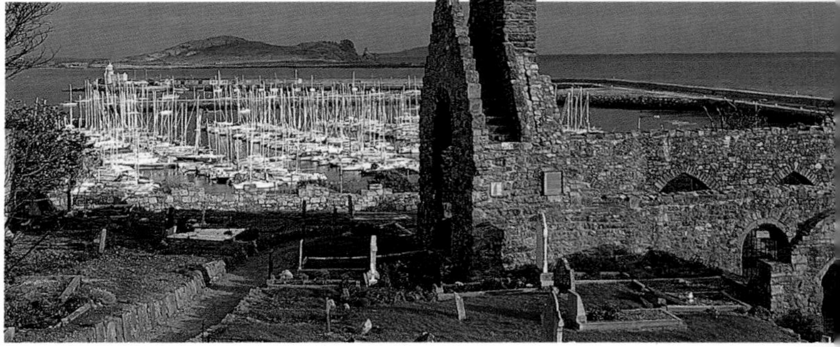

1–2

Turn left out of Howth's DART station, past the harbour full of fishing boats. The **waterside** is dotted with fishmongers and restaurants, and you may even catch a glimpse of a seal in the water as the vessels unload the day's catch.

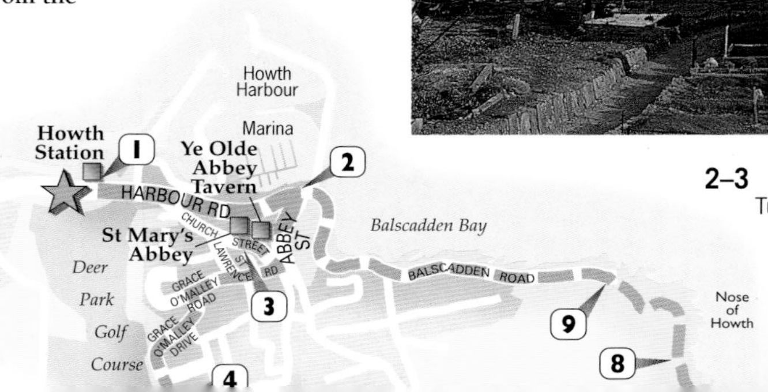

2–3

Turn right up Abbey Street. Climb the steps on the right beside **Ye Olde Abbey Tavern** to reach the ruins of **St Mary's Abbey** (above), once a medieval seat of learning famed throughout Europe, now little more than a roofless 16th-century shell. The view from here over

Howth Harbour

Marina

Howth Station

Ye Olde Abbey Tavern

HARBOUR RD

ABBEY ST

CHURCH STREET

St Mary's Abbey

LAWRENCE RD

GRACE O'MALLEY ROAD

Deer Park

Golf Course

Balscadden Bay

BALSCADDEN ROAD

Nose of Howth

4–5

Turn right at the top, and go up a ramp beside Ballylinn (No 53). Ascend a grassy slope, keeping to the right for a little way, and then up the steep slope through the trees. Continue south, keeping the rugby pitches well to your left and the golf course to the right, until you are parallel with the top of the golf course.

5–6

Bear right around the top edge of the golf course, following the path into trees. Cross the

Hidden Treasure

The knobbly white quartzite rocks ringing Shielmartin's crown were placed here 2,000 years ago to mark the burial place of Crimhthan Niadhnair, warrior king of Ireland. Helped by his goddess wife, Nar of the Brugh, he mounted attacks on the newly arrived Romans in Britain, returning home laden with plunder. Ireland's Eye, the craggy offshore islet in Howth Bay, was his look-out post, hence the name. No one knows where the king buried his booty: some say it's on Shielmartin, others claim it lies on the promontory under the Baily Lighthouse.

Howth Marina and the crooked, crab-like claws of the harbour break-waters is sensa-tional. Howth (rhyming with "both") takes its name from the Norse word *Hoved* meaning "head". The penin-sula was an island until comparatively recent times when an isthmus of gravel formed, thereby connecting it to the mainland.

3–4

Go down Church Street into Abbey Street and take the next turning right up St Lawrence's Road. In 100m (110 yards), continue straight ahead along Grace O'Malley Road, then left up Grace O'Malley Drive. On a bend, to the right of Woodlands (No 37), keep going straight up a path to rejoin the road. Continue for 20m (22 yards), then turn right up a flight of steps beside Robin Hill House.

Whitewater Brook

Baily Lighthouse

Doldrum Bay

ROAD

CARRICKBRACK

▲154m Ben of Howth

Golf Course

Howth

▲171m Shielmartin

Kissing gate

6

7

0 — 500 metres
0 — 500 yards

next golf course (keeping a good look-out), and climb the slope ahead. This steep, rough path, flanked by dense purple heather, leads to the top of **Shielmartin**. At 171m (561 feet), this is the highest point on the peninsula. Pause awhile to enjoy the views: to the south is Dublin Bay, the city and the Wicklow Mountains beyond; to the north is the scenic coastline of Portmarnock, Lambay Island and Ireland's Eye, and, on a clear day, the distant Mountains of Mourne.

6–7

A clear path leads from here southwards down to **Carrickbrack Road**. Turn left, and 300m (330 yards) later cross the road and pass through a kissing gate (by the "Dangerous Cliffs" sign). This path leads through rocks down to the shoreline.

7–8

Turn left and follow the narrow, rocky cliff path for 8km (5 miles) all the way round Howth Head, past the **Baily Lighthouse**, admiring the sensational seascape of deep-cut coves, lichen-clad stacks and stumps, brackery slopes and hedgerows of fuchsia and gorse as you go. **Howth Head** boasts more than half the total of Ireland's indigenous plant species and an abundance of wildlife and seabirds. Remember also James

Joyce and *Ulysses*. It was here that Leopold Bloom proposed to Molly "the day we were lying among the rhododendrons on Howth Head in the grey tweed suit and his straw hat, the day I got him to propose to me, yes…"

8–9

Continue along the coastal path back into Howth. As you turn the corner at the **Nose of Howth**, your efforts will be rewarded by breath-taking views of the northern coastline and Ireland's Eye. This harshly weathered islet was formerly a monastic settlement but nowadays only seabirds live here. In summer there are regular boat trips here from Howth Harbour.

9–1

Return along the coastal path to Howth, back down to the harbour and the DART station.

Taking a Break

There are many pubs, cafés and restaurants in Howth. The **Big Blue** in Church Street makes an ideal light lunch spot, affording great harbour views. Or, for a special meal, try **Aqua** (right on the fishing pier), one of Dublin's top fish restaurants.

Organised Tours

On Foot

Dublin is compact and therefore easy to explore on foot. Here are some of the best organised walking tours.

The **Historical Walking Tour of Dublin**, led by Trinity College history students, provides an excellent introduction to the city – a guide to the cultural, religious and political history of Dublin, exploring such key events in Irish history as the influence of the American and French revolutions, the Potato Famine of 1845–48, the 1916 Rising and the current Peace Process. (During June, July and August three further historical walks are offered: A Terrible Beauty – the Birth of the Irish State 1916–1923: The Gorgeous Mask – Dublin's Architecture; and Unmanageable Revolutionaries – Women in Irish History. Tel: 01 878 0227 for details.)

Perhaps the best way to get a feel for the city's alcohol-fuelled literary heritage is to try a **Literary Pub Crawl**, where two actors perform recitations and anecdotes from Joyce, Beckett, Yeats, O'Casey, Behan, Lavin and Wilde between visits to four of the pubs made famous by these writers. A great combination of street theatre, *Guinness* and *craic!*

In a similar vein, the **Musical Pub Crawl** is led by two professional musicians who perform tunes and songs while telling the story of Irish music, between visits to a range of famous musical pubs including Gogarty's and the Norseman and climaxing in a lively musical *seisiún*.

If modern music is more your style, try the self-guided **Rock 'n' Stroll Trail** which takes in such venues as O'Donoghue's, the Bad Ass Café (where Sinéad O'Connor once waitressed), Merchant's Arch (where Phil Lynott played in his pre-Thin Lizzy days) and the Windmill Lane recording studios, made world famous by U2. Call into Dublin Tourism in Suffolk Street (▶ 37) to pick up a booklet.

If you're feeling brave, try the **Walk Macabre**, a unique tour with members of the Trapeze Theatre Company. You visit scenes of murder and intrigue in the elegant surrounds of Georgian Dublin and are introduced to the works of famous writers who excelled in horror, the supernatural and the bizarre.

By Bus

Hop-on hop-off tours of the city centre give an excellent overview of Dublin and are a convenient means of sightseeing, with stops near most of the major attractions. Each open-top bus has a tour guide who delivers a witty and informative commentary as you go, and your day ticket enables you to hop on and off as often as you wish throughout the day. Look out for red City Sightseeing buses, green-and-cream Dublin City buses, and black-and-gold Gray Line buses.

Dublin boasts the world's only **Ghostbus**. This is no ordinary tour. The blood-red curtains inside the bus are drawn closed to ward off evil spirits lurking outside and those on board are transported to the spooky side of the fair city, far removed from the tourist attractions of daytime Dublin. Actors bring the gaslight ghosts, fiends and phantoms of the city's troubled past to life, with highlights including Dracula's

origins, torch-lit body-snatching in St Kevin's graveyard and a visit to the haunted steps of St Audoen Protestant church.

On the Water
Viking Splash Tours's award-winning trip aboard a bright yellow, reconditioned World War II vintage amphibious vehicle takes you from land to water to see the city sights. Children love it…especially the big splash into the historic Grand Canal Basin. For something racier, **Sea Safari** will take you on a one-hour high-speed, adrenalin-packed tour in a large RIB (rigid inflatable boat) around Dublin Bay and the surrounding coastline from Skerries to Killiney Bay, with regular sightings of seals, porpoises and other wildlife.

Contact Details

Ghostbus Tour
Start: Dublin Bus office, 59 O'Connell Street, D1
Duration: 2.25 hours
Tel: 01 873 4222 (booking essential); www.dublinbus.ie
Mon–Fri 8pm, Sat–Sun 7pm and 9:30pm. Expensive.

Historical Walking Tour of Dublin
Start: Trinity College (front gate), D2
Duration: 2.5 hours
Tel: 087 688 9412;
www.historicalinsights.ie
May–Sep daily 11, noon, 3; Apr, Oct daily 11; Nov–Mar Fri–Sun 11. Expensive (pay on the day).

Hop-on Hop-off Bus Tours
Start: O'Connell Street, D1
Duration: 1.5–1.75 hours
Tel: 01 873 4222;
www.irishcitytours.com;
www.dublinbus.ie
Daily 9:30–5:30. Expensive.

Literary Pub Crawl
Start: Upstairs at the Duke pub, Duke Street, D2
Duration: 2 hours
Tel: 01 670 5602;
www.dublinpubcrawl.com
Apr–Nov nightly 7:30 and Sun noon; Dec–Mar Thu–Sat 7:30pm, Sun noon and 7:30. Arrive by 7pm. Expensive (book at Dublin Tourism, Suffolk Street, D2, or pay on the door).

Musical Pub Crawl
Start: Upstairs at the Oliver St John Gogarty pub, Fleet Street, D2
Duration: 2.5 hours
Tel: 01 478 0193;
www.musicalpubcrawl.com
Apr–Oct nightly 7:30; Nov, Feb–Mar Fri–Sat 7:30pm. Expensive.

Sea Safari
Start: Dublin City Moorings (opposite Jurys Inn Hotel), Custom House Quay and Malahide Marina, D1
Duration: 1 hour
Tel: 01 855 7600 or 01 806 1626; www.seasafari.ie
Daily 11–5. Expensive

Walk Macabre
Start: Main gates of St Stephen's Green, D2 (opposite Planet Hollywood)
Duration: 2 hours
Tel: 087 677 1512 (booking essential);
www.ghostwalk.cjb.net
Daily 7:30pm (operates only if there are more than 5 people). Expensive.

Viking Splash Tours
Start: Bull Alley Street, beside St Patrick's Cathedral, D8
Duration 1.5 hours
Tel: 01 707 6000;
www.vikingsplashtours.com
Mid-Feb to Dec: ten tours per day (phone for details). Expensive (book at Dublin Tourism, Suffolk Street, D2, or pay on departure).

Practicalities

GETTING ADVANCE INFORMATION

Websites

- www.visitdublin.com
- www.visit.ie/Dublin
- www.ireland.ie
- www.ireland.com
- www.timeout.com/dublin

Tourist Offices

In Dublin
Dublin Tourism Centre
Suffolk Street, D2
☎ 1850 230330
Email: information@
dublintourism.ie

In Dublin
Irish Tourist Board
Baggot Street Bridge, D2
☎ 01 602 4000

BEFORE YOU GO

WHAT YOU NEED

● Required
○ Suggested
▲ Not required

Entry requirements differ depending on your nationality and are also subject to change without notice. Check prior to a visit and follow news events that may affect your situation.

	UK	Germany	USA	Canada	Australia	Ireland	Netherlands	Spain
Passport/National Identity Card	●	●	●	●	●	▲	●	●
Visa (waiver form to be completed)	▲	▲	▲	▲	▲	▲	▲	▲
Onward or Return Ticket	▲	▲	▲	▲	▲	▲	▲	▲
Health Inoculations (tetanus and polio)	▲	▲	▲	▲	▲	▲	▲	▲
Health Documentation (► 174 Health)	○	○	●	●	●	●	●	●
Travel Insurance	○	○	○	○	○	○	○	○
Driving Licence (national)	●	●	●	●	●	●	●	●
Car Insurance Certificate	○	○	△	△	△	○	○	○
Car Registration Document	●	●	△	△	△	●	●	●

WHEN TO GO

Dublin – seasonal high temperatures

[ ] High season   [ ] Low season

JAN	FEB	MAR	APR	MAY	JUN	JUL	AUG	SEP	OCT	NOV	DEC
8°C	8°C	10°C	13°C	15°C	18°C	20°C	19°C	17°C	14°C	10°C	8°C
46°F	46°F	50°F	55°F	59°F	64°F	68°F	66°F	63°F	57°F	50°F	46°F

☀ Sun   ☁ Cloud   🌧 Wet   🌦 Sun/Showers

Temperatures are the **average daily maximum** for each month. The best time to visit Dublin is between April and October, when the weather is at is best, although the city is popular to visit at any time of year. **Peak tourist months are July and August**; book accommodation early. Christmas and the New Year are also popular. During November to March, the weather can be change-able. Most of the time it is cloudy, and frequently wet, dark and dreary. Autumn is generally fine, with a high percentage of crisp days and clear skies. Be pre-pared for rain at some time during your stay, no matter when you visit, but try to accept the rain as the Irish do – as a "wet blessing".

In the UK
Tourism Ireland
103 Wigmore Street
London W1U 1QS
☎ 0800 039 7000

In the USA
Tourism Ireland
345 Park Avenue
New York, NY 10154
☎ (212) 418-0800

In Australia
Tourism Ireland
5th Level
36 Carrington Street
Sydney, NSW 2000
☎ 02 9299 6177

GETTING THERE

By Air There are **direct scheduled flights** from Britain, mainland Europe and North America to Dublin Airport (tel: 01 814 1111; www.dublin-airport.com). The Republic's national airline is **Aer Lingus** (tel: 0845 084 4444 (UK); 01 886 6705 (Dublin); www.aerlingus.com). **Other scheduled carriers include** Continental Airlines, Delta, British Airways, British Midland, Air France, Alitalia, Iberia, Lufthansa and SAS.
Ryanair (tel: 0871 246 0000 (UK); 01 609 7800 (Dublin); www.ryanair.com) offers cheap rate fares from destinations around Europe.
For current flight details of all main carriers, services, ticket prices, special offers and packages, check with your travel agent, the airlines or the internet.
Approximate flying times to Dublin: from the UK (1–2 hours), from mainland Europe (2–4 hours), from USA/Canada (6–9 hours), from Australia/New Zealand (12-plus hours)

By Ferry Ferries from the UK sail into Dublin and Dun Laoghaire, 14km (9 miles) south of the city.
Irish Ferries (tel: 08705 171717 (UK); 1890 313131 Dublin; www.irishferries.com) operate daily between Dublin Port and Holyhead (1 hour 50 minutes by fast ferry; just over 3 hours by cruise ferry). Their MV *Ulysses*, the world's largest car ferry, has capacity for 2,000 passengers, and a crossing time of just over 3 hours between Dublin Port and Holyhead.
Seacat (tel: 08705 523523 (UK); 1800 551743 (Ireland); www.seacat.co.uk) operates a daily Seacat Rapide hovercraft service from Dublin Port to Liverpool; crossing takes 4 hours.
Stena Lines (tel: 0870 570 7070 (UK); 01 204 7777 (Dublin); www.stenaline.ie) operate a daily fast service (99 minutes) between Dun Laoghaire and Holyhead, or a 3.5-hour crossing from Dublin Port to Holyhead.

TIME

Ireland runs on Greenwich Mean Time (GMT) in winter. From late March until late October, clocks are put forward 1 hour, and British Summer Time (GMT +1) operates.

CURRENCY AND FOREIGN EXCHANGE

Currency The monetary unit of the Republic of Ireland is the Euro (€). Notes are in denominations of €5, €10, €20, €50, €100, €200 and €500, and coins in denominations of €1 and €2, and 1, 2, 5, 10, 20 and 50 cents.
Travellers' cheques are the most convenient way to carry money. All major credit cards are widely recognised.
Exchange Most **banks and bureaux de change** will exchange cash and travellers' cheques. Banks tend to offer better exchange rates than store, hotels and bureaux de change, although the latter generally stay open later than banks. You will find booths at the airport, sea ports, some department stores and some railways stations. Many banks have ATMs for cash withdrawal.

TIME DIFFERENCES

GMT	Dublin	London	USA (NY)	USA (West Coast)	Sydney
12 noon	12 noon	12 noon	← 7 am	← 4 am	→ 10 pm

WHEN YOU ARE THERE

CLOTHING SIZES

UK	Dublin	USA	
36	46	36	
38	48	38	
40	50	40	
42	52	42	Suits
44	54	44	
46	56	46	
7	41	8	
7.5	42	8.5	
8.5	43	9.5	
9.5	44	10.5	Shoes
10.5	45	11.5	
11	46	12	
14.5	37	14.5	
15	38	15	
15.5	39/40	15.5	
16	41	16	Shirts
16.5	42	16.5	
17	43	17	
8	34	6	
10	36	8	
12	38	10	
14	40	12	Dresses
16	42	14	
18	44	16	
4.5	38	6	
5	38	6.5	
5.5	39	7	
6	39	7.5	Shoes
6.5	40	8	
7	41	8.5	

NATIONAL HOLIDAYS

1 Jan	New Year's Day
17 Mar	St Patrick's Day
Mar/Apr	Good Friday
Mar/Apr	Easter Monday
First Mon May	May Holiday
First Mon Jun	June Holiday
First Mon Aug	August Holiday
Last Mon Oct	October Holiday
25 Dec	Christmas Day
26 Dec	Boxing Day

OPENING HOURS

○ Shops   ● Post Offices
● Offices   ● Museums/Monuments
● Banks   ● Pharmacies

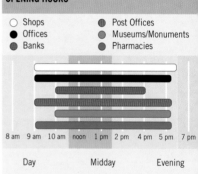

8 am 9 am 10 am noon 1 pm 2 pm 4 pm 5 pm 7 pm

Day   Midday   Evening

Shops In addition to the times shown above, some shops open on Sundays. Late-night shopping is on Thursday with most shops remaining open until 8pm.
Banks Most banks are closed on Saturdays. Some banks remain open till 5pm on Thursdays.
Post Offices Some city-centre post offices open on Saturday mornings. The General Post Office on O'Connell Street is open Mon–Sat 8–8 (7pm for parcels), Sun 10–6.
Museums Hours vary according to the season, so always phone ahead to avoid disappointment. Some attractions have shorter opening hours on Sundays.
Pharmacies Pharmacies display a list of pharmacies open at night and on Sundays. O'Connell's Late Night Pharmacy, 55 O'Connell Street Lower, is open Mon–Fri 7:30am–10pm, Sat 8am–10pm, Sun 10–10.

POLICE 999 or 112

FIRE 999 or 112

AMBULANCE 999 or 112

PERSONAL SAFETY

Until recently, street crime was rare in Dublin, but petty crime is now on the increase. To be safe:

- Keep watch of handbags and wallets in public places.
- Keep valuables in your hotel safe.
- At night, avoid Phoenix Park, poorly lit alleys and side-streets.
- Keep cars well secured and avoid leaving property visible inside.
- The national police in Dublin (and the rest of the Republic) are called Garda Siochána (pronounced shee-*kaw*-nah) in black-and-blue uniforms.

Police assistance:
 999 or **112** from any phone

ELECTRICITY

The power supply is 240 volts AC. Sockets generally are the UK type, with three square pins. Overseas visitors should bring a voltage transformer and plug adaptor.

TELEPHONES

Public phone booths are grey or green-and-white, and take coins, credit cards or phone cards (sold at post offices and newsagents). For national telephone enquiries,

dial 11811.
For other countries, dial 11818.
For national operator assistance dial 10.
For the international operator, dial 114.
All numbers preceded with 1800 are toll-free.

International Dialling Codes

Dial 00 followed by:

UK:	44
USA/Canada:	1
Ireland:	353
Australia:	61
Germany:	49
Netherlands:	31
Spain:	34

POST

Post boxes and vans are painted green. You can buy stamps from post offices, machines or some newsagents.
Post offices are usually open Mon–Fri 9–5:30, Sat 9–1.

TIPS/GRATUITIES

Most restaurants now include a service charge, so a tip is not necessary, although it is customary to round up the bill, leaving an extra 5 per cent of the total.

Restaurants (service not included)	10%
Bar service	No
Taxis	10%
Tour guides	€1
Porters	50 cents
Chambermaids	discretion
Lavatories	small change

EMBASSIES

UK
01 205 3700

USA
01 668 8777

Netherlands
01 269 3444

Germany
01 269 3011

Australia
01 676 1517

HEALTH

 Insurance Nationals of EU and certain other countries can get medical treatment at reduced cost with the European Health Insurance card (not required by UK nationals). Medical insurance is essential for all other visitors.

 Dental Services EU nationals, or nationals of other countries with which Ireland has a reciprocal agreement, can get dental treatment within the Irish health service with the European Health Insurance card (not needed for UK nationals). Others should take out private medical insurance.

 Weather June and July are the sunniest months, although July and August are the hottest. If visiting at these times, cover up, apply a good sunscreen and drink plenty of fluids.

 Drugs Pharmacies are easily recognised by their green cross sign. Their highly qualified staff are able to offer medical advice on minor ailments, provide first-aid and prescribe a wide range of over-the-counter drugs.

 Safe Water Tap water is safe to drink. Mineral water is widely available, but often expensive.

CONCESSIONS

Senior citizens Senior citizens (over 60) are entitled to discounts on transport and most admission fees on proof of age.

Students Students under 18 are entitled to reduced entrance in some museums and galleries. Be sure to carry some form of identification.
Holders of an International Student Identity Card can buy a Travelsave Stamp which entitles them to travel discounts including 50 per cent reduction on the Irish bus and train network (Bus Éireann and Iarnród Éireann), and Irish Ferries between Britain and Ireland. Contact your local student travel agency for further details. The Travelsave Stamp can be purchased from USIT, 19–21 Aston Quay, O'Connell Bridge, Dublin 2 (tel: 01 602 1777).

TRAVELLING WITH A DISABILITY

Helpful booklets are *Guide for Disabled Persons, Buildings for Everyone* and *Accommodation Guide for Disabled Persons*, available from the National Disability Authority at 25 Clyde Road, D4 (tel: 01 608 0400).

CHILDREN

Well-behaved children are generally made welcome everywhere. Many sights, museums and attractions offer reductions. Baby-changing facilities are excellent in the newer museums and attractions but can be limited elsewhere.

LAVATORIES

Public facilities are usually clean and safe. Most galleries and museums have lavatories and most bars, hotels, fast food outlets and department stores will let you use theirs.

CUSTOMS

The import of wildlife souvenirs sourced from rare or endangered species may either be illegal or require a special permit. Before purchase you should check your home country's customs regulations.

The Irish Language

Irish Gaelic (*Gaelige*) is the Republic's official language, and is commonly referred to as "Irish". It is a Celtic language, closely related to the Gaelic languages of Scotland, Wales and Brittany in France. Irish remained the country's everyday language right up to the time of the Great Famine, when the ensuing mass emigration robbed the country of a very high proportion of its native Irish speakers. In Dublin today, Irish is spoken by some and understood by many, but English is the language which predominates.

The past decade has seen a resurgence of interest in the Irish language. It can be studied at Trinity College and several other universities; children are taught it throughout their school days, and must sit an examination in it as part of their leaving certificate.

USEFUL PHRASES

Yes **Sea**
No **Ní hea**
Hello **Dia dhuit**
Goodbye **Slán agat/Slán leat**
Please **Más é do thoil é/Le do thoil**
Thank you **Go raibh maith agat**
Today **Inniu**
Tomorrow **Amárach**
My name is... **...is ainm dom**
How much does it cost? **An mó atá air?**
Where is...? **Cá bhfuil...?**
Hotel **Óstan**
Restaurant **Bialann**
Menu **Biachlár**
Beer **Beoir**
Wine **Fíon**
Lavatories **Seomra folctha**
Entrance **Bealach isteach**

Exit **Éalú**
Open **Oscailte**
Closed **Dúnta**

Monday **Dé Luain**
Tuesday **Dé Máirt**
Wednesday **Dé Céadaoin**
Thursday **Dé Déardaoin**
Friday **Dé Haoine**
Saturday **Dé Sathairn**
Sunday **Dé Domhnaigh**

NUMBERS

One **Aon**
Two **Dó**
Three **Trí**
Four **Ceathair**
Five **Cúig**
Six **Sé**
Seven **Seacht**
Eight **Ocht**
Nine **Naoi**
Ten **Deich**
Twenty **Fiche**
Forty **Daichead**
One hundred **Céad**
One thousand **Míle**

INTERNET CAFÉS

Central Café
6 Grafton Street, D2
Tel: 01 677 8298; fax: 01677 8299; www.centralcafe.ie;
Open: Mon–Fri 8am–11pm; Sat 9am–11pm; Sun 10am–11pm.

does not compute
Unit 2 Pudding Row, Essex Street West, Temple Bar, D8
Tel: 01 670 4464; fax: 01 670 4474; www.doesnotcompute.ie;
email: info@doesnotcompute.ie
Open: 24 hours.

Global Café
The Basement, 8 Lower O'Connell Street, D1
Tel: 01 878 0295; fax: 01 872 9100; www.globalcafe.ie;
email: info@globalcafe.ie
Open: Mon–Fri 8am–11pm; Sat 9am–11pm; Sun 10am–11pm.

Recommended Reading

The Irish literary tradition is one of the most illustrious in the world, famous for four Nobel Prize winners and for many other writers of international renown. Below is a selection of books written about Dublin as well as some of the most popular fictional and biographical works by Dubliners and set in the city:

BOOKS ON DUBLIN

Douglas Bennett *An Encyclopaedia of Dublin* (Gill & Macmillan, Ireland). Everything you could ever want to know about the capital.

Maeve Binchy *Dublin 4* (Poolbeg). Four short stories observing the decadent lifestyle of the fashionable D4 district south of the Liffey.

Max Caulfield *The Easter Rebellion* (Gill & Macmillan, Ireland). The definitive guide to the events of 1916.

Tony Claton-Lea and Richie Taylor *Irish Rock* (Gill & Macmillan, Ireland). Development of the Dublin music scene.

Peter Costello *Dublin Churches* (Gill & Macmillan, Ireland). An illustrated record of more than 150 churches.

John Cowell *Dublin's Famous People: Where They Lived* (O'Brien Press). Brief biographies of local luminaries.

Maurice Craig *Dublin 1660–1860* (Liberties Press). An historical account of an evolving city.

Joss Lynam *Easy Walks Near Dublin* (Gill & Macmillan, Ireland). Forty short, straight-forward walks in and around Dublin.

Peter Zöller *Dublin: Portrait of a City* (Gill & Macmillan, Ireland). A photographic account of the city.

BOOKS SET IN DUBLIN

Brendan Behan *Borstal Boy* (Arrow). A romanticised biography, portraying the author's involvement in the Republican movement and his early years in prison.

Dermot Bolger *Father's Music* (Flamingo). A psychological thriller set in Dublin.

Christy Brown *My Left Foot* (Minerva). This is an unsentimental autobiography of Christy Brown, who was born with cerebral palsy, in which he describes his life as part of a large Southside family.

Philip Casey *The Fabulists* (Lilliput). A compelling love story set in contemporary Dublin.

Roddy Doyle *The Commitments* (Minerva), *The Snapper* (Penguin), *The Van* (Penguin). A witty trilogy centred on the north Dublin Rabbitte family written in a vernacular style.

James Joyce *Ulysses* (Penguin). An epic account of 24 hours in the life of hero Leopold Bloom, set in Dublin, at the same time drawing parallels with Homer's *Odyssey*.

Iris Murdoch *The Red and the Green* (Penguin). A fictional account of an Anglo-Irish family at the time of the Easter Rising.

OTHER NOTABLE WORKS BY DUBLINERS

Samuel Beckett *Molloy, Malone Dies, More Pricks than Kicks* and *The Unnameable*
Brendan Behan *The Hostage*
Maeve Binchy *Circle of Friends, The Lilac Bus* and *Light a Penny Candle*
Roddy Doyle *A Star Called Henry*
James Joyce *Portrait of the Artist as a Young Man* and *Dubliners*
Bram Stoker *Dracula*
Jonathan Swift *Gulliver's Travels*
Oscar Wilde *The Picture of Dorian Gray*

Streetplan

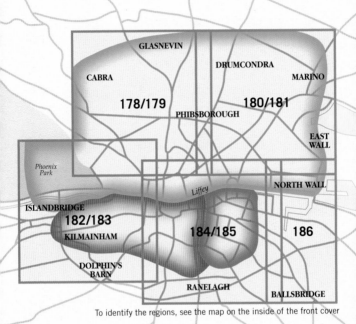

GLASNEVIN

DRUMCONDRA

CABRA

MARINO

178/179

180/181

PHIBSBOROUGH

EAST
WALL

*Phoenix
Park*

NORTH WALL

Liffey

ISLANDBRIDGE

182/183

184/185

186

KILMAINHAM

DOLPHIN'S
BARN

RANELAGH

BALLSBRIDGE

To identify the regions, see the map on the inside of the front cover

Key to Streetplan

.... Main road

.... Other road

≡≡≡≡≡ Footpath

┊┊┊┊┊ Pedestrian street

———— Rail line

Park

Important building

▪ Featured place of interest

𝑖 Information

| 0 | 100 | 200 | 300 | 400 | 500 metres |
| 0 | 100 | 200 | 300 | 400 | 500 yards |

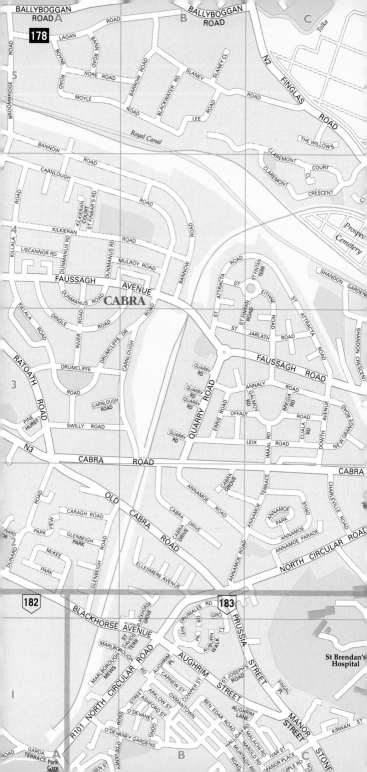

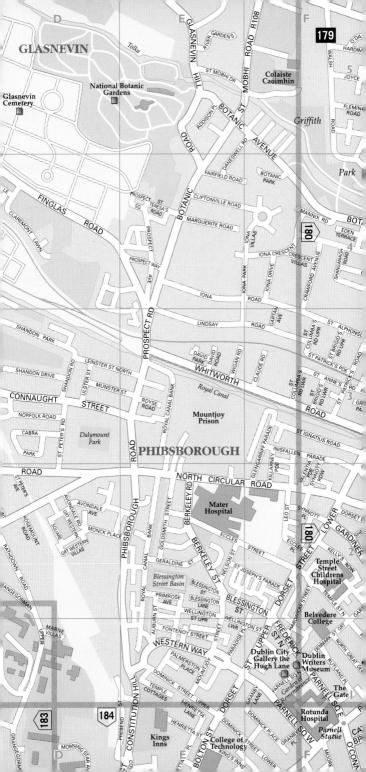

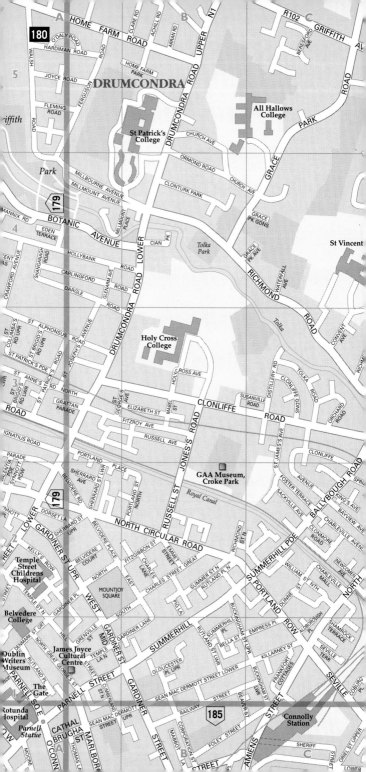

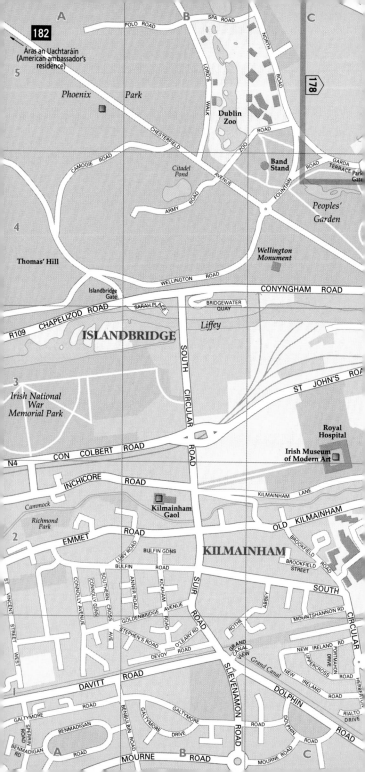

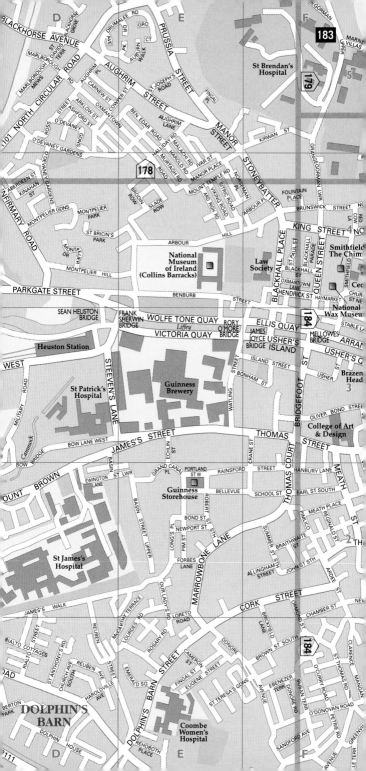

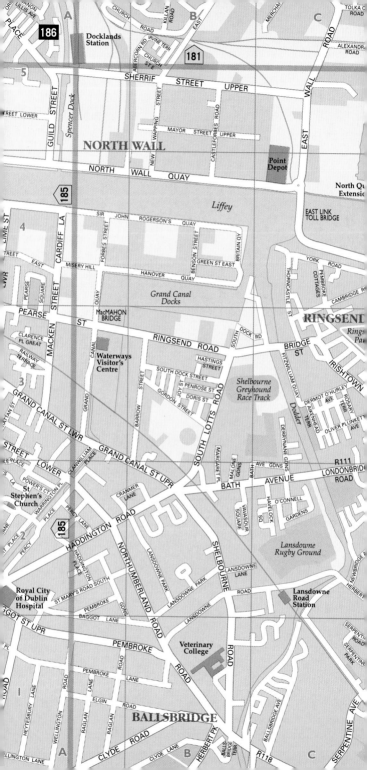

STREETPLAN INDEX

Ave	Avenue
Br	Bridge
Cl	Close
Cres	Crescent
Ct	Court
Dr	Drive
E	East
Gdns	Gardens
Grn	Green
Grt	Great
La	Lane
Lwr	Lower
Mem	Memorial
Mid	Middle
N	North
Pde	Parade
Pk	Park
Pl	Place
Rd	Road
S	South
Sq	Square
St	Street
Terr	Terrace
Upr	Upper
W	West

Picture credits

Abbreviations for terms appearing below: (t) top; (b) bottom; (l) left; (r) right;
(c) centre.

The Automobile Association wishes to thank the following photographers, libraries
and associations for their assistance in the preparation of this book:

Front and Back Cover: (t) AA Photo Library/Slide File; (ct) AA Photo Library/S L Day;
(cb) AA Photo Library/S Whitehorne; (b) AA Photo Library/S L Day; Spine: AA Photo
Library/S Whitehorne (©Guinness 1940)

ALLSPORT K LTD 32; BRIDGEMAN ART LIBRARY 90t *Book of Kells* (The Board of
Trinity College, Dublin, Ireland), 90b *Book of Kells* (The Board of Trinity College,
Dublin, Ireland), 94l "Lady writing a letter with her Maid" by Jan Vermeer (National
Gallery of Ireland, Dublin, Ireland), 94r "View of Kilmallock" by John Mulvany
(National Gallery of Ireland, Dublin, Ireland), 95 "The Toy Seller" by William
Mulready (National Gallery of Ireland, Dublin, Ireland), 98/9 The Tara Brooch
(National Museum of Ireland, Dublin, Ireland), 99 The Ardagh Chalice (National
Museum of Ireland, Dublin, Ireland); COLLECTIONS 3(ii) (Michael Diggin), 89b
(Michael Diggin), 96 (Julian Nieman), 102br (Michael St Maur Shiel), 141 (Michael
Diggin); CORBIS 121t; M DIGGIN 173bl; EMPICS 32/3; MARY EVANS PICTURE
LIBRARY 10t; GUINNESS 57; HULTON ARCHIVE 11, 14b, 24/5, 24l, 25r, 55b, 56, 66,
92; IMAGEFILE 16b, 22t, 29br, 33; IMAGESTATE 26tl; IRISH MUSEUM OF
MODERN ART 70; HUGH LANE GALLERY 130 (Perry Ogden. © The Estate of
Francis Bacon); REDFERNS MUSIC PICTURE LIBRARY 26tr; REX FEATURES LTD
12t, 25br, 27; VIKING ADVENTURES 71

The remaining pictures are held in the Association's own library (AA PHOTO
LIBRARY) and were taken by STEVE DAY with the exception of the following:
L Blake 14t, 34t; C Coe 16/17, 16t, 19, 26l, 144/5; C Hill 150; S Hill 173t; S McBride
2(iv), 23b, 29bl, 55, 58, 68/9, 68b, 83, 87t, 92/3; M Short 15b, 29tr, 31, 74, 89t, 104t,
142/3, 145, 146; Slide File 22b, 58/9, 134b, 147; W Voysey 102l, 126r; S Whitehorne
2(iii), 3(iv), 8t, 8bl, 15t, 49, 52, 53t, 68l, 87c, 101, 124, 126/7, 127, 135, 154l, 158,
164, 166, 169, 173br; P Zoeller 143, 148/9

The author wishes to thank the following for their assistance:
Catherine McCluskey, Jenny Finnegan and Olivia Owens of Dublin Tourism; John
Lahiffe of the Irish Tourist Board; and Stephen and Gary Duffy.

Questionnaire

Dear Traveler

Your comments, opinions and recommendations are very important to us. So please help us to improve our travel guides by taking a few minutes to complete this simple questionnaire.

Send to: Spiral Guides, MailStop 66, 1000 AAA Drive, Heathrow, FL 32746–5063

Your recommendations...

We always encourage readers' recommendations for restaurants, nightlife or shopping – if your recommendation is added to the next edition of the guide, we will send you a FREE AAA Spiral Guide of your choice. Please state below the establishment name, location and your reasons for recommending it.

_____

_____

_____

_____

_____

Please send me AAA Spiral_____

(see list of titles inside the back cover)

About this guide...

Which title did you buy?

_____ **AAA Spiral**

Where did you buy it? _____

When? m m / y y

Why did you choose a AAA Spiral Guide? _____

_____

_____

_____

Did this guide meet your expectations?

Exceeded ☐   Met all ☐   Met most ☐   Fell below ☐

Please give your reasons _____

_____

_____

_____

continued on next page...

Were there any aspects of this guide that you particularly liked?

_____

_____

_____

_____

_____

Is there anything we could have done better?

_____

_____

_____

_____

_____

About you...

Name (Mr/Mrs/Ms) _____

Address _____

_____

_____ **Zip** _____

Daytime tel nos. _____

Which age group are you in?

Under 25 ☐   25–34 ☐   35–44 ☐   45–54 ☐   55–64 ☐   65+ ☐

How many trips do you make a year?

Less than one ☐   One ☐   Two ☐   Three or more ☐

Are you a AAA member? Yes ☐   No ☐

Name of AAA club _____

About your trip...

When did you book? ☐ ☐ / ☐ ☐   **When did you travel?** ☐ ☐ / ☐ ☐

How long did you stay? _____

Was it for business or leisure? _____

Did you buy any other travel guides for your trip? ☐ Yes   ☐ No

If yes, which ones? _____

_____

Thank you for taking the time to complete this questionnaire.